PARENTING
— FOR A —
PEACEFUL HOME

HOW TO OVERCOME ANGER AND LEAD BY A LOVING EXAMPLE

DREW TUPPER

Copyright © 2021 Drew Tupper

All rights reserved. No part of this book may be reproduced, stored, or transmitted by any means—whether auditory, graphic, mechanical, or electronic—without written permission of both publisher and author, except in the case of brief excerpts used in critical articles and reviews. Unauthorized reproduction of any part of this work is illegal and is punishable by law.

This book is dedicated to Emmett, Pearl, and Kiku. I am eternally grateful to you and what you have taught me. I love you.

INTRODUCTION

"Children learn more from what you are than what you teach."
—W.E.B. DuBois

Why This Book?

When my kids were young, I wanted a parenting book that would tell me how to deal with my anger and impatience. I want something straightforward and written in plain English. I wanted a book written, not from theory, but from lived experience. I wanted real life perspectives and strategies that would work for me.

I suppose I wrote this book for me. This became the parenting book I wish I had had.

I wrote this book to share with other parents who can relate to my story of being angry, impatient, and reactive. I want to help make parents' lives easier and more enjoyable.

I also wrote this book for children who don't get a say in the parenting they receive. Their lives and futures depend on it, but they don't get a choice. They simply get what they get.

And I wrote this book for our collective future. I believe that we as parents have a great responsibility to give our children the best of ourselves so that they can flourish, and our world can flourish. Children literally are the future.

What I've imagined is this: Healthy, well-adjusted children, the kind who were cared for in calm and loving ways. Then, I imagine those children growing up into adults and having children of their own, being raised in the same way as their parents. The ripple effect will be huge. What you implement from this book won't just impact you as a parent now, it will also impact your children when they become parents, and their children's children.

Imagine a world like that! What would happen if more and more children were raised in calm and connected homes? The possibilities are endless. So many of our current challenges in the world come from how we relate to each other and the earth. If healthy relating is learned at home, that is what would become the norm around the world. I imagine more peace, love, and caring for each other and the earth. I think that's worth striving for.

It's NEVER too late to start doing this. It's always worth it. It's never too late to build stronger, healthier, and more compassionate connections with your children. It's worth starting at any point.

> "The best time to plant a tree was 20 years ago. The second-best time is now." —Chinese Proverb

What Kind of Parenting Book is This?

This is a practical book with methods that can be applied in your real life. I'm not an academic, physician, nor am I a writer. I am a dedicated parent who wants the absolute best for my kids. I'm also a parent coach who helps other parents give the best of themselves to their children. I figured some things out that changed my and my children's lives for the better, and I want to share them with you. The goal of this book is to provide you with a simple yet powerful framework to become a more patient and positive parent. It is a handbook, really. I share with you the exercises that helped me become more patient and less reactive. I believe this book will help you create a stable, loving, and enjoyable home environment for your family.

Using my own personal experiences, I'll take you through my journey of how I went from angry and impatient to being much calmer and more positive.

I will show you how I did the following:

- Gained awareness of myself and my emotions
- Regulated my heightened emotions
- Calmed myself in general
- Valued myself and took care of myself
- Better understood my children and their needs and emotions
- Modeled to my children how to calm themselves
- Used conflict as an opportunity to model, connect, and problem solve
- Loved and forgave myself

Other books will tell you how to deal with bedtime, mealtime, gaming, and other challenging behavior. While those books can be helpful, this is not that kind of book. Rather, this book is about the *inside job* of parenting. First and foremost, it is about becoming a *self-regulated* parent. It approaches parenting holistically. If the internal environment of the parent is healthy and positive, the home environment will also be healthy and positive. This is the main premise.

How to Use This Book

Take your time reading this book. Working through this material is a process. Answer the questions and do the exercises in each chapter.

The questions and exercises work best when approached with intentionality and curiosity. Be open and honest. Don't sugar-coat the difficult things or downplay the truth. Be vulnerable and speak from your heart. You'll get out of this book (and the exercises) what you put into it.

Apply what you read to your life. Books, lessons, and lectures are great, but the learning must be applied. Real life is the real teacher. Make your life the classroom—this is where you'll learn your most important lessons.

There are different ways to use this book: alone, with a partner, or in a group. If you do it on your own, get a journal and write your answers to the questions and reflections to the exercises. In fact, journal your answers to the exercises even if you do the book with a spouse, friend, or as part of a group. It will provide a reference to go back to when you need it.

A Book Based on My Own Experience

This book is about my own experience and my story. My story includes my identity and the lens through which I perceive the world. I am a middle-class North American, neurotypical white male, with neurotypical children.

The observations and suggestions in this book may not be applicable to everyone. Not all parents, children, and situations are like mine. However, by sharing my story I have helped many parents and families to date, and I feel compelled to continue to do so.

This book centers around changing the parent's internal environment, perspective, and behavior. I understand that there are factors that influence a parent's ability to change his/her own behavior and there are factors that influence a child's ability to react to changes in parenting. Some things are due to medical or other issues beyond anyone's control.

This book is not about those things. This book is about the things that I changed and how it worked. This book is about the things that I began doing differently as a parent, and how those changes affected my children's lives and development for the better. If this is useful to you, great. If not, that's okay, too. Do what works for your family. Please seek all professional care applicable to your situation.

My story also includes where I came from. I grew up in the suburbs of Ontario in the 1980's. I had good friends, enjoyed playing sports, and did well in school. My home life was generally positive. We played games together, had good conversations, had lots of laughs, and would go on family vacations that were fun. I was loved and well-provided for and really appreciate what my parents gave me.

Being a child of the 80's however, I was also spanked, shamed, grounded, yelled at, and parented/educated in the style of the time. This book is not a condemnation of my parents or anyone else. I know my parents were trying to do the best for me. I know that all parents are doing the best they can with the backgrounds, information, and tools they have.

This book is about how I am choosing to do things differently. It's okay to want to do things differently. Most of our parents also did things at least a little different than their parents. It's okay to want to improve. We can do this while still appreciating where we came from.

Get Really Honest

"I was a great parent, until I had children."
—Anonymous

I Was Out of Control

Before I had kids, I assumed I'd be a great parent. My wife and I had been married for almost 5 years, together for 10. Our relationship was stable, and we were both intelligent and capable enough to handle having a family. We were in good health. We were both wise enough (33 and 30) to not enter into parenting in a naive way. That is what I thought, anyway.

I didn't see any reason why parenting would be particularly difficult. In the past, if I had tried hard enough at something, I was able to do it. So, I assumed I'd be a competent dad. However, parenting didn't come easily to me. I found it surprisingly difficult.

I had the most challenging time with my son's behavior, especially if it was counter to what I thought should happen. This started to happen around 1 ½ years of age when children start to express their own will. I found myself frequently wanting to control and correct his behavior. I found myself getting worked up when I thought that his behavior was inappropriate. It felt like my son was poking at my sore spots. This is when I started getting frustrated, angry, and short-tempered.

Don't get me wrong—having a family has been the best thing that has ever happened to me. It certainly hasn't been all bad, not by a long shot. I love my children to the moon and back and we've had tons of fun together. However, truth be told, I knew that I wasn't being the best dad I could be. I was too erratic and sensitive to what was age-appropriate behavior.

I felt surprised and confused at my emotions and reactions. I had never expected that I would react the way I did, or that so many intense emotions would rise to the surface in parenting. Far too often, I'd yell and lose control. To make matters worse, I had no idea when my lid would flip. I was caught off guard by my own emotions. I was so discouraged. I was not ready for this part of parenting. This was not how I thought it would be. I was afraid of failing my children, of hurting them.

I knew some of my outbursts went too far. I spanked my child, I held him down on the ground, I grabbed him, pulled him, pushed him, and yelled as loud as I could at him. I found myself struggling greatly to control my anger. I did not understand how this emotion and behavior could live inside of me.

One time, I remember angrily holding my son down, trying to get him to get dressed. I can still hear his little 3-year-old voice saying, "Daddy, you are hurting me." It kills me to remember that, to imagine what this little boy might have been thinking and feeling. It pains me to write about this and relive those moments. He was so little when I did this. It must have been terrifying for him to see his dad get so angry and hurt him like that. I was the one that was supposed to be loving him and protecting him. He was innocent and helpless. As I look back, I almost don't recognize that man who would hurt his young child with such loss of control.

And it's not just the physical harm that I engaged in- I yelled, blamed, and shamed. Negative words flew out of my mouth far too often. I was demeaning, threatening, and coercive. I did all this without planning to do so. Before I knew it, I would be yelling toxic things at my son like. "What the hell were you thinking?!" It was as if I was possessed by something that I didn't want to admit was me.

Looking back now, I certainly feel sad for my son. He didn't deserve any of that. No child does. What children primarily need is safety and a loving connection. I didn't know that I was stuck on an autopilot that threatened this safety and connection. I was lost. I wish I had known better, but I honestly don't think I did. I don't think any parent is in their right mind when they hurt their child.

Calling Parents In

This is what is happening around the world. Parents are acting in ways that they don't want to be acting. They are losing control of themselves and hurting the people most important to them. It is upsetting and frustrating to be in this position. It feels like the ultimate failure.

Don't get confused. I am not here to blame, shame, or judge myself or others. That doesn't work, and it never will. I am sharing my truth to bring this out into the light. Although it is not entirely comfortable to hold myself accountable like this, it serves a purpose. I knew that if I was having these problems, others were, too. My intention is not to belittle you or your efforts. This book is about empowering and uplifting parents to be the parents they really want to be. To do that, we must be honest first. Honesty is key.

No More Behind Closed Doors

There is a "behind closed doors" phenomenon that occurs in parenting. We can become completely different people in our homes when no one else is watching.

When we leave home and go out in public, accountability on our behavior automatically increases. We go out into the world where others are watching, where there are norms and rules that are enforced. We go to the bank, to the store and to work, where there are clear standards of behavior. There are varying degrees of consequences for not adhering to norms. Accountability is built into the social fabric, both formally and informally.

However, when we come home and shut the door, accountability on our behavior drastically decreases. People are not watching. For the most part, the parent creates the norms, and the rules. The parent creates the standards of behavior for him/herself. As parents, we are responsible for regulating ourselves. It takes a strong and skillful person to not take advantage of this position of power.

This is why it is so important for the parent to develop self-awareness and self-regulation. The home is the place where we need to be the most accountable and consistent in our behavior. Yet, it is the place where the worst of the parent can come out. I've acted in ways at home that I would never act in public or at work. This is not okay. It is understandable, but not okay.

If you are acting in ways that you know are not okay, the first step is to acknowledge it, then it's time to do something about it. Our children are counting on us.

No More Sweeping Things Under the Carpet

In the beginning, after an outburst, I tried to downplay what I had done. I'd act kinder for a few days until I was sure that we were "okay". I'd secretly convince myself that I hadn't done any damage to my son or our relationship.

Eventually, I'd see him smile; I'd see him playing. He'd give me a hug and a kiss, and I'd think, *Everything is okay here, we're good.* As time passed, however, I found it harder to ignore that things were not okay. I was beginning to see the negative impacts of my parenting. I could sense that our relationship was damaged. Things were changing. His behavior seemed increasingly erratic, anxious, and angry as I pressed on with the parenting that I knew.

No More Shifting Blame

For a while, I made excuses. I shifted responsibility onto my son. I'd blame him for making me angry. I would have said that it was his behavior that was causing me to lose control. *Weren't parents just always right anyway? A parent didn't need to alter his behavior; the child did, right?*

Now I understand that having a higher standard for a child's behavior than an adult's behavior is backwards. Holding my young son responsible for my behavior was not great parenting. It was me giving away my own power and accountability. I get that now.

I am ultimately responsible for me and my behavior. I choose my behavior. No one else makes me do anything, and most certainly not a young child.

Old Habits Die Hard

Even with the recognition that I was not fully being the parent I wanted to be, a stubborn part of me still held on to the idea that being controlling and harsh with my child was somehow an important part of parenting. It was hard to let go of my negative tendencies. They died hard.

I had a hard time shaking the idea that teaching lessons required some amount of negativity or fear. *If I didn't scare my child, how would he learn? How would I get his attention if I didn't yell or get angry?*

Part of me believed that negative discipline practices were valid parenting practices. After all, I turned out "fine". I believed in the idea of tough love. I was worried that if I got too soft, my kids would turn out to be entitled, weak, and disrespectful. Yes, I was operating from fear.

Honestly, I didn't really know what else to do. I did not know of viable alternatives. I didn't have any other tools. I didn't know how to parent in a different way that could merge love, patience, and effectiveness. I felt overwhelmed.

I have been at the precipice of this ledge many times. Can I trust a new way? Can I accomplish what I want? Will this work out? I get it. Old patterns die hard.

But I am writing this book to tell you **Yes**. Yes, there is a better way. Yes, it is effective. It will help you accomplish all that you want, and more.

The Getting Honest Exercise

My first step towards being less reactive and more mature was to address the illusion that things were okay. In essence, the first step was to stop kidding myself and to start being honest. Here's your chance to do the same.

Questions (Remember to Journal Your Answers)

1. What are your behaviors that are reactive and/or negative?

2. Why is this a problem? What problems is your behavior creating?

3. What happens if you keep on with this behavior? What is the impact on your children? What is the impact on your relationship with your children?

4. Is there a big enough reason for you to read this whole book, to write out every exercise and commit yourself to learning and growing? What is that reason and why does it matter?

5. What is your plan for when you forget or lose sight of this reason?

Thank you for being honest. This work is straightforward, but not always easy. You'll get frustrated as you try new things. You'll have to revisit and replace your old beliefs. You'll have to continue being honest with yourself. You'll have to stay focused and consistent. You'll fail at times and be humbled. You'll question yourself, and you may be questioned by others. People may judge you as you start to practice this more mature way of parenting.

If you are ready and willing to take full responsibility for your behavior, read on. If you're not sure, that's okay. You can put the book down and come back to it later when you *are* ready.

If you are ready, then great. You've just taken the first and most important step to becoming the kind of parent you can be proud of.

Lead by Example

"…a leader is anyone who takes responsibility for finding the potential in people and processes, and who has the courage to develop that potential."
—Brené Brown

Parenting Is a Leadership Role

Whether I liked it or not, I was thrust into a leadership position the day my first child was born. Together with our partners, we create the home environment that our children are growing up in. They watch our example and feed off our energy every day. We are responsible for their development.

Before becoming a parent, I had not fully appreciated the importance of parenting as a skill like leadership, a skill to be practiced and learned. I only realized the magnitude of my role as a parent around the time my first child was two or three.

Every day he looked to me, listened to me, and mimicked me. With the birth of my children, my actions and words mattered a whole lot more. I knew this because I could see it. I could not ignore that my actions and behavior deeply impacted my children. The only kind of parenting that made sense was one of leading by example.

Children are observant. You cannot get away with trying to teach one thing and live another. It won't really matter what lessons you try to teach in any one moment if those lessons are not consistent with your behavior. The lessons will not stick, and even worse, trust will erode, and the relationship will be damaged.

For my children to be their best, *I* must be my best. I cannot give my children something I do not have. I must *be* that which I wish to teach in all aspects of life. If I want my children to be patient, *I* must be patient. If I want my children to be the best versions of themselves, I must strive to lead *by my best example* in everything that I do. This was a tough truth to realize.

Yes, there is a lot of responsibility here, and there is so much opportunity. As a parent, I had no choice whether or not I was going to teach by example, but I did have a choice about what my example would be.

Looking to the Best Mentors and Leaders

When I realized how much my behavior was affecting my children, I aspired to live as a good example. I wanted to serve my family to the best of my ability. I wanted to do my part in helping my children be their best. One important thing that helped me was to look to those in my life that had been good leaders and mentors, those who were dedicated to bringing out the best in others. I remember one such leader named Dave Dineen. He led a youth leadership program that I attended. He led by such an amazing example. His presence and his being were the content of the program, as far as I am concerned. Sure, we did activities geared towards the growth of our leadership skills, but the way this man walked, talked, and encouraged us all to be our best was the real lesson for me.

This is what I have seen in my life: Good leaders and mentors created relationships that were less about directing obedient followers or "mini-me's" and more about helping their mentees become leaders in their own lives. These good leaders created positive environments that respected the uniqueness of the individual. As a result, they were trusted, listened to, and appreciated. Their teams were creative, collaborative, and empowering. As I reflected, I remembered that it felt both enjoyable and purposeful to be in this kind of environment.

I noticed that these leaders created this environment by doing two things. The first, is that they acted with a high degree of personal responsibility. This means that they had a defined set of values and lived by them. They were accountable for their actions and owned their mistakes when they happened. The second thing I noticed is that they genuinely cared about the well-being and growth of those they led. The best leaders created strong relationships of mutual caring and respect. They treated their teams as they wanted to be treated.

I wanted to be like these leaders and mentors and wondered if I could apply their same approach to parenting. I reflected on the various teams I'd been on, and what worked and what didn't. I made notes, and then I took what I thought could be effective and applied it to my parenting. It turned out to be *highly* effective.

Questions:

1. What kind of team do you like to be on? What kind of mentorship/leadership do you appreciate? What kind of environment brings out the best in you? Make a list of the things that have helped you be your best and give your best to a team.

2. Do you think your children would respond well to some of your answers to question 1? Why do you think they would?

3. How do you think your children have learned from your example already?

4. What would you like to teach your children and how could you teach that through your example?

Realizing I Was Not a Good Leader

It's clear to me now that the best leaders lead by example and don't micromanage. They build trust. Good leaders create a supportive, open environment for everyone to learn and grow in.

On the other hand, I notice that ineffective leaders focus on controlling those under them. They focus on blaming their team for "bad behaviors" and try to limit and punish rather than encourage a growth mindset, whereby team members learn from mistakes rather than feel ashamed of them.

Unsuccessful leaders lacked self-awareness, self-regulation, direction, and effective communication skills. Ineffective leaders seemed insecure and distrustful. They seemed to limit the potential of people and demotivate them. Sadly, I realized that in the mentoring of my children, too many of my behaviors were in the "ineffective leader" column.

I became inspired by this honest look at my leadership and felt motivated to embody more of these qualities that, in turn, create cultures that bring out the best in everyone.

Good Mentors/Leaders:

- live with integrity and model the behaviors they wish to see
- listen well and genuinely care about team members
- are motivated by a vision bigger than themselves
- create and form teams with shared values and vision
- create a culture of positivity and possibility
- are empathetic and understanding
- create an environment of emotional safety and belonging
- empower team members
- promote open, two-way communication and welcome feedback
- are interested and invested in the lives of team members
- have a non-judgmental, encouraging tone
- are assertive, not aggressive or passive
- make clear agreements, rather than rely on assumptions and expectations
- use mistakes as learning opportunities
- help team members develop their skills
- help team members to contribute by using their strengths
- celebrate wins and value effort
- use humor
- are curious
- are vulnerable
- help the team stay optimistic and focused on the vision

Emotional Intelligence

"The most effective leaders are alike in one crucial way: they all have a high degree of what has come to be known as **emotional intelligence**. It's not that IQ and technical skills are irrelevant. They do matter, but…they are the entry-level requirements for executive positions. My research, along with other recent studies, clearly shows that emotional intelligence is the sine qua non of leadership. Without it, a person can have the best training in the world, an incisive, analytical mind, and an endless supply of smart ideas, but he still won't make a great leader." (Daniel Goldman, Harvard Business Review, 1998)

There's humility and vulnerability in good leadership. In my study of good leaders and mentors, I noticed a quality of not just intellect, but emotional intelligence. Good leaders understand themselves, their own strengths, weaknesses, feelings, thoughts, and values. They understand the people around them as well. It seems as if acquiring emotional intelligence is essential to becoming a good leader and mentor.

Relationship Capital: Connection Leads to Cooperation

Like mentorship, parenting is a relationship, one based on trust. Trust is damaged when a mentor is volatile, inconsistent, judgmental, out of integrity, and discounts the feelings and needs of his mentees. When safety and connection get compromised in this way, children cannot trust the parenting leadership. It's a natural phenomenon to not respect or listen to those who don't seem to have your best interests at heart. It makes sense, rationally and intuitively, not to not trust a leader like that.

When children sense that the leadership is consistent, helpful, and forgiving, cooperation is the *automatic* result. By becoming more in control, consistent, and encouraging in my actions, I have gained the trust of my children and therefore more of their cooperation.

Questions:

1. What type of person do you generally trust? What are the behaviors that earn your trust?

2. Are you willing to listen to and cooperate with those who you trust? Why?

3. How would a leader lose your trust? Do you think this is similar to how a parent could lose the trust of a child? How so?

There are a few basic communication skills that I started to use at home that immediately improved my communication with my children. As my success in this area grew, I started to feel more competent and less overwhelmed. As for my children, they calmed down and started to listen to me more. Our home environment became more stable and enjoyable.

Here is what you can do to improve your communication with your children:

- **Connect before you direct**. Connection governs cooperation. Be interested in your child and what your child is doing. Show curiosity. Ask them questions about their lives or what activity they are engaged in. *Enter their world* and build some rapport before asking them to do things or giving instructions.

- **Inject loving presence.** This is particularly important if you lean towards a more aggressive or direct way of speaking. Get close, use eye contact, use your child's name, and touch your child gently on the shoulder before you speak. Speak more from your heart. Imagine you were speaking kindly to a close friend.

- **Watch your tone.** Get rid of the "parent tone" in favor of a respectful and connecting tone of voice. Watch your body language too. Get rid of rolling eyes, furrowed eyebrows, sighs, hands on hips, gritting your teeth, and shaking your head. Being mindful of your non-verbal signals is really challenging, but super important. So much is communicated through body language.

- **Aim for balance of voice.** When asking your child to do something, be assertive and encouraging, not aggressive, but not passive either. Attempts at being soft and non-threatening can sometimes backfire. Parents who slip into passive communication can get ignored. Getting ignored can cause frustration and often leads to yelling.

- **Speak clearly and concisely.** Don't give lengthy, meandering requests or lectures. Slow down. Breathe. Think before you speak. Choose your words very wisely. Your words will be more valuable and carry more weight this way.

- **Be clear about your intention.** If you are giving an instruction, do not make it into a question. Many parents suffer from up-speaking and/or adding lots of "Okays?" to the end of their instructions. If you are asking a question, ask a question. If you are giving an instruction, give an instruction. Be careful not to confuse the two...*okay*? If you want to check for comprehension, ask: "What did you hear/understand?"

- **Be positive.** If you are giving an instruction, word it in the positive instead of the negative. For example: "Hang your jacket here, please" Versus: "Don't leave your jacket on the floor!" This lets children know what *to* do, instead of what *not* to do.

- **Demonstrate the skill.** Reinforce by demonstrating what you want done. "Hang your jacket here *like this*. Now you try it. Great, thanks."

- **Offer to help.** Many young children need help getting started and staying on track. Calmly offering, "Can I help?" has resolved countless challenges and potential conflicts.

- **Be calm.** (If it's not an emergency) Walk slowly across the room to speak to your child in a calm voice. Yelling across rooms runs the risk of training your child to answer you only after you have yelled.

- **Try giving your child some choice and control.** They'll feel less need to be defiant if choice is a part of their world. This was especially true with my strong-willed child. "Would you like to do this first or that first"?

- **Deliberately notice and then appreciate your Children.** For example: "You put your toys in the toy box. Thank you. That was helpful."

- **Listen** to your children when they want attention or when they want to speak to you. If you can't listen at that exact moment, take 10 seconds to pause what you are doing, face them, make eye contact, and tell them when you will be able to pay attention.

The last point is HUGE: Listen to your children when they want attention or when they want to speak to you. Acknowledge and recognize their bids for attention. When this happens, make eye contact, and get face-to-face. Listen intently and show genuine interest. Ask questions and be curious. It models listening and cooperation, big time.

Remember that leading/teaching by example is the main way that kids learn. So, listening intently to them is how you teach them to listen. When we let our children know that we hear them and understand them, children will learn how to do this, too, and they will consequently reward us with a level of trust that will strengthen the relationships immensely.

Question:

1. Do you think any one of the above approaches could work for you at home? Which ones, and why?

2. Do you know of any other ways good leaders communicate that might also be effective at home? Think of how you like to be spoken to. Do you think your child(ren) would respond well to this? How so?

3. Much of good communication comes down to tone. Describe the overall tone or energy you have noticed in good leaders or mentors. Do you think your child(ren) would respond well to this? If so, why?

Your Family as an Organization

As parents, we are leaders and mentors, and our children will respond to us in much the same way that adults respond to organizational leaders. The leadership determines the success of the organization. The responsibility for a smooth-running family rests squarely upon the shoulders of the leaders of the family, not the children.

Blaming children for an uncooperative or stressed-out family situation is like blaming the interns for not ensuring the overall success of an organization. As many mistakes as the interns make, it is not their responsibility to run a smooth and successful organization.

Poor leaders blame the ones they lead, while good leaders take responsibility. What had kept me somewhat blind to the potential benefits of leadership in parenting was an old way of thinking that suggests that children are the problem. I hadn't appreciated the extent to which parents really are leaders, and children really are people who respond to the quality of the leadership.

For those who lean more toward the side of gentle and peaceful parenting, don't worry, I'm not talking about a dictatorship. I am not talking about a "power over" leadership. I am talking about the kind of leadership Brené Brown describes in her book *Dare to Lead*: "Daring leaders work to make sure people can be themselves and feel a sense of belonging."

There is potential for so much progress in the world of parenting when it is treated as leadership or mentorship. It allows one to approach parenting as a skill that can be studied, learned, and practiced. It allows one to use the lessons they already know from their work and adult life and apply them at home. I found a calming confidence in this. I discovered that I knew more than I had realized.

The two simple and powerful questions I ask myself again and again are:

What kind of team do I like to be on? Am I creating that kind of environment at home?

Questions:

1. As a leader at home, what are your current strengths?

2. As a leader at home, what is your area for growth?

3. What would happen if you approached parenting like leadership and endeavored to learn and use the skills of good leadership at home?

Create a Vision

> "If you don't know where you are going,
> you might wind up someplace else."
> —Yogi Berra

Visualize What You Want

In the early years, I parented from how I was feeling in the moment, rather than from goals or vision or values. My behavior depended on my mood and level of stress and was therefore erratic. When I felt secure and confident, my parenting was usually constructive and encouraging. When I felt stressed or overwhelmed, my insecurities would get the best of me, and I would not act in the best interest of my children. I would be short and even angry. At some point, I realized I no longer wanted to leave my parenting approach to how I was feeling in the moment. I wanted to develop more consistency and a framework, or guiding light, for my parenting. This framework would support me and pull me through even the toughest times.

So, I created a vision for where I wanted to go. The power of the mind is astonishing. Visualizing helped me flesh out and define what I wanted to accomplish. It also had the effect of acting as a magnetic beacon. A phenomenon occurs when you create a vision. Once you experience a vision that resonates with you, you get pulled toward the vision. This is why professional athletes, top performers, and business leaders use visualization: It works.

Questions to Prepare You for Creating Your Vision:

1. Think back on how you were raised. Would you like to parent your children in a similar way? Why or why not?

2. Have you noticed any automatic or reactive parenting tendencies you have that aren't in line with how you'd want to parent?

3. If you created a vision for the way you want to parent, how do you think this could help you?

My Objections to Crafting a Vision.

There was something that made it difficult to commit to defining a vision; it was my ego. My egoic self wanted to reserve the right to parent how I felt like parenting at any given moment. I wanted to feel in control. I didn't want structure, or anyone telling me what to do, not even my higher self.

Creating a vision meant that I would then need to act in alignment with the vision. Or not, and then feel the sting of abandoning my true vision. I would have to be consistent in my behavior to have a hope of achieving what I wanted. I could not hope and plan for one thing while acting in ways counter to that. This level of accountability was uncomfortable for me.

Furthermore, my ego convinced me that *I should have somehow already known how to parent*. My ego judged me as weak for admitting I was lost and needing structure. I, of course, was a bit lost. Admitting that what I was currently doing wasn't working was hard, but it paved the way for growth.

Are you feeling any objections toward creating and pursuing a vision? How can you resolve those objections?

Here is how I dealt with my own objections:

I told my ego to take a back seat. I had to get over myself. There was no other way around it. If I wanted the best for my kids, I had to stop protecting myself and my insecure interests. I could no longer pretend that I was above this work. I had to be willing to feel uncomfortable. I had to loosen my grip of what I thought was control. I had to humble myself. I had to try new things and do things that might be challenging.

And, I had to believe in myself.

I told myself that I had learned other new things in my life, and that I could learn this too. I could learn how to be patient, positive, and consistent in my behavior.

Here are the visioning exercises that helped me gain focus. Do them and reap the benefits.

Exercise: What the Ideal Future Looks Like

Find a quiet place and/or a place that inspires deeper thought.

Imagine your children as emerging adults getting ready to leave home. Imagine that they are about to set off into the world. Paint a picture in your mind of your future family. Imagine your parenting had gone really well. You are happy with how you parented and very proud of your children. You feel successful. Imagine this best-case scenario. Take some time to think about it. To make it more vivid, imagine a specific scene. For example, you can imagine standing in the kitchen talking, sitting down for dinner, or going for a walk. Write down and describe what you see and feel. To add more detail, answer the following questions:

- *What do you notice in your future vision that stands out to you?*
- *What do you notice about your children in this vision that indicates to you that the future is good?*
- *What is present in the interaction between you and your children to let you know that things have gone well? What is your relationship like with your child?*
- *How do you think your children feel? Why do they feel this way?*
- *What do your children look like when you look at their faces, bodies, and body language?*
- *What about you? What do you see when you look at you?*
- *What does it feel like to imagine this ideal vision and to know that you have played a big part in creating it?*
- *Describe how you have grown so that you were able to model what you wanted to teach.*

Journal your answers and discuss with your partner, or group, if you have one.

Below is a short description of what I saw when I looked into the future. Do the exercise above for yourself, before reading mine.

For me, the answer was simple. I saw us all being happy and healthy. I saw everyone thriving. We all loved each other and supported each other. My kids felt comfortable and confident in who they were. They were excited about life and about the challenges ahead. They believed in themselves and were ready to pursue their dreams or were already doing so.

The relationship my wife and I had with our kids was one of trust and openness. We were there to act as a sounding board, coach, and of course, provide comfort when needed. To imagine a future like this felt warm and hopeful. My vision provided the clarity I needed to help move us toward a good future. If I could work toward this, then I would know I'd be doing my best.

Are you on track to create this vision? If not, where are you headed if the status quo continues?

My personal answer was **no**. I was not on track. When I connected the dots from what I was currently doing to my future vision, I was doubtful that I'd achieve even close to what I had imagined. I knew I wasn't doing my part to raise the happiest and most confident individuals I could. This realization hit me hard.

In fact, I had seen signs of my parenting having the *opposite* effect and that *I* was creating a future that I didn't want. Earlier in the book, I shared some of the detrimental ways I was parenting. In short: I knew that what I was doing wasn't going to yield the result I wanted -- for me, my wife, or my children. Not only was I in danger of not raising happy and confident children, I wasn't likely to have a close and trusting relationship with them in the future. I needed to pay attention closely and change my behavior so that I could give us all a strong shot at achieving the best possible future.

What is in your way of creating this vision?

For me, the main thing was, well…me. I could clearly see that I was getting in my own way. Specifically, my behavior was getting in the way. My reactive and unpredictable behaviors would not create the right kind of environment for my kids to thrive.

Exercise: Get Focused

I instinctively began to ask myself some questions to correct my course. I sat with these questions and dug deep to find the answers. I focused on creating a framework for what I needed to do.

Here are the questions I asked myself. I've included my answers below for you to see, but please look at them after answering for yourself.

1. What are the 2 or 3 things from the vision that you'd most like to see come true?

2. What are the behaviors you must stop if you want to create this vision? How are you getting in your own way to achieve what you most want?

3. What are the behaviors you must regularly act out if you want to create this vision?

4. Who do you have to be?

Here are my answers:

1. This may have been the hardest question to answer, and it has yielded the most important information for me. There were so many things I thought I had to accomplish as a parent. I felt a lot of pressure, so it was hard to focus on just two or three things.

I had to sit with this question for a while, but the core of what I wanted to accomplish was this: I wanted my parenting to be infused with love and kindness. I wanted our interactions to be based in love and real respect. I wanted my children to know that they were loved and accepted no matter their behavior, no matter the mistake. This was the bedrock upon which I wanted to live my life and build my family.

The second thing was that I wanted to empower my children to be the most authentic versions of themselves possible. I wanted to help them believe in themselves and their own strengths. I imagined this love and empowerment leading to great things. To me, it seemed like everything else I envisioned flowed from these two core essentials: love and authenticity. Kids raised in this way would feel happy, worthy, capable, confident, generous even. Not every day, maybe, but most days – at least kids raised this way would have a bedrock of love and truth to draw on in hard times. They could rest in the knowledge that no matter what, they were loved, and that their truth resided within their own heart. I imagined that kids who felt like this would also be loving and respectful to others, while standing up for themselves and what they believe in.

This is what I wanted my children to have experienced by the time they left home. If I could accomplish this, I would have succeeded. I've noticed that in talking to many other parents, their vision of parenting success isn't all that different from mine.

2. What did I have to stop doing? I had to draw a line in the sand. There were things I absolutely could not do if I wanted to create the vision I imagined. I could not use fear and blame to help me achieve what I wanted. I could not be physically aggressive, spank, yell, or shame my kids. I had to start parenting and teaching through love and empowerment, and I had to be consistent in that approach.

3. What did I have to do to achieve this vision? I realized that if I wanted my kids to feel loved and empowered, I had to be loving and empowering to my kids (and to myself). But what did that actually mean?

I imagined **loving** looking like this: being calm, patient, respectful, a good listener, empathetic, affectionate, understanding, and forgiving.

To me, being **empowering** meant helping my children understand themselves, learn how to speak for themselves, and how to do things for themselves. Empowerment entailed being curious together, guiding gently, involving them in an encouraging way, and giving them appropriate responsibility.

4. Who did I have to become?

The simple answer is that I had to become what I wanted to teach. If I wanted to infuse love into the relationship and into the heart of my child, I needed to be loving with myself. I had to be calm, patient, respectful, a good listener, empathetic, affectionate, understanding, and forgiving…with myself. Self-love *must* be at the forefront. There is no way around it. Our primary practice for relationships is how we treat ourselves internally.

Furthermore, if I wanted to empower my kids, it would mean that I had to live an empowered life myself. It would be modeled by living my own truth. It involved setting an example of taking responsibility for myself and my mistakes, trying my best, and allowing myself to go for what I want, even though I might fail. Empowerment is living with a growth mindset. It is defining ourselves not by our failures, but by what we can learn from our experiences.

What About Everything Else?

Obviously, there are other things I want to accomplish as a parent. For example, I want to keep my kids safe, healthy, well-nourished, and provide them with lots of opportunities to play, learn, and grow. It's not that I ignore these other things, it's that they are held in the context of my overall vision.

Here is the question that now guides my parenting philosophy, when interacting with my kids:

How can I behave in this situation so that it is loving and empowering toward my children?

What is a question you could ask yourself to remind yourself of your vision?

When I took the time to figure out what I really wanted, parenting became both easier and more purposeful. It felt like there were *fewer* things to worry about and my energy could be directed to what mattered most. This provided me with significant peace of mind.

I lacked focus before I clarified the most important things to concern myself with. The small things would get just as much attention as the bigger, more important goals. The results of having a never-ending laundry list of things to accomplish and not being able to prioritize was two-fold: I felt tons of stress, and I lost focus on what was important.

So, do yourself a favor. Make peace with yourself, knowing that you can still be a good parent without checking all those boxes. They're imaginary anyway.

There's so much going on in parenting and in life that prioritizing your desired outcomes and acting accordingly is not only ideal, but necessary. The bottom line is that we cannot come close to achieving our vision if we lose focus, get overwhelmed, or act in ways that are counterproductive to what we desire to achieve. For example: dinner table manners, going to bed on time, and contributing to family chores are reasonable things to teach. However, sacrificing the greater vision to accomplish these is counterproductive to your ultimate aim. Acting in alignment with your vision allows you to take care of these things with ease.

Likewise, getting caught up in a power struggle about chores where I yell or force my child into compliance would be winning the battle but losing the war. Not smart.

So, I opt out of what is tempting. I opt out of the quick power trip. I come back to my vision, and I ask myself: "How do I teach this in a way that is loving and empowering?"

Resetting and Putting the Vision into Practice

If you realize that you have been acting out of alignment with your vision or that you are off track, it's time to get refocused.

A good way to do this is to acknowledge it, to name and to address it -- with yourself, *and with your children*. The following exercise is something I do with my family.

Exercise: Repair and Reset

Have a family meeting where you take ownership of your behavior to date, and you involve your children in your vision of what you want for them and for your family. A child as young as 3 or 4 years old can understand this and will add value to the conversation. This is a great opportunity for connection and empowerment.

My conversation sounded something like this:

"I want to apologize for something. I have not been the parent that I have wanted to be. Here is why. I have been hurting you and yelling at you. That's not right and you don't deserve to be treated like that. You are good kids, and you deserve to be treated kindly and respectfully. I am sorry that I have treated you like that.

"It must have been scary and frustrating for you when I acted like that. Would you like to tell me about how it felt?" (pause and listen)

"It's not your fault that I got angry. I get angry because of me and because I have a hard time controlling myself. I didn't ever learn

how to feel my emotions or how to talk about them or control them. I am learning now."

"I am hoping we can all learn together. We can work on keeping ourselves calm and kind. Does that sound good?"

"I am going to be trying really hard. You guys are so important to me. Mom is going to be helping me. And you can remind me too. If you don't like what I'm doing or how I'm speaking to you, you can tell me. You can say 'Daddy, I don't like that.' I will take a deep breath and listen to what you are saying. I might need to take a break or go to a different room to calm down and remember how I want to behave.

"What do you think? Do you have any questions?"

"I have a hope (vision) that we can have a loving and enjoyable family and that I can help you two become happy and confident people. What do you think about that? Is there something you would like to add? What else would you like to experience in our family?"

"Do you have any suggestions for how we can accomplish what we want?"

Learn to Be Humble

Resetting and repairing is something I do **regularly**. I am not perfect, and I continue to make mistakes. When I do, I own my mistakes and repair with my children. Not every mistake requires a big, long reset conversation, but not acknowledging that you have made a mistake…is well, *a big mistake.*

Here is the great thing about repairing. You can apologize and address things that have happened in the past. It could be quite healing. It can feel humbling, but it's worth it. Honesty and humility have taken me far.

Repairing is also a great modeling opportunity of how to take responsibility. As parents we can try to force our children to apologize...thinking that it's our job to "teach" manners. However, a forced apology has no real empathy behind it, it is issued out of fear rather than true caring, and it sounds that way. When we demonstrate a real apology, we demonstrate real empathy, caring, and personal responsibility and our children will follow suit.

Get on the Same Team

In the reset exercise, you'll notice that I asked for help. This is something you can do. You can take ownership of your own challenges and ask for support. You can tell your partner (and kids) where you are likely to have a misstep and what they can do to help you get back on track. It was hard to admit my own challenges. I felt a bit like a failure, but in the end, the well-being of my kids took priority. My ego had to sit down.

In essence, I gave my wife the go-ahead to step in if she saw me going down the wrong road of negativity. We worked out how to do that, what words to say and such. I think it was a tap on the shoulder and something to the effect of "Can I help?" This asking for help allowed me to own the process and feel empowered. If I hadn't done this and she offered to step in, it might have felt like judgment that I wasn't doing things the right way. Use your support. Ask for help. Claim your process and your own growth.

Practice Self-Awareness

"Know thyself."
—Socrates

Becoming Emotionally Intelligent

I looked to the teachings of emotional intelligence to create a home that was less reactive, and more loving and empowering. Emotional intelligence is "the capacity to be aware of, control, and express one's emotions, and to handle interpersonal relationships judiciously and empathetically." (Dictionary.com -Oxford Languages)

It was hard to leave my old way of parenting behind and set off on this new path. I constantly questioned my own logic. Can I really parent like this? Can children really learn the lessons they need to learn without fear? At the time, I hoped so. Now, I know so. I made the shift with success. I have found that not only are lessons learned, but they are learned better.

Self-awareness is the foundation of emotional intelligence; one's emotional intelligence cannot evolve without it. Self-awareness is the key to understanding yourself and then managing your emotions and behaviors from that understanding.

Without self-awareness, there is no emotional intelligence, and without emotional intelligence, there is no mature and encouraging parenting.

Developing self-awareness was the beginning of my being able to gain self-control so I could lead by example. No matter how many books I read or how hard I hoped for something different, I couldn't effectively and consistently manage my own behavior until I developed a practice of self-awareness.

The practice of self-awareness shifted my entire perspective and is the foundation for mature and skillful living, leading, and parenting.

What is Self-Awareness?

Simply put, self-awareness is the practice of being an observer of oneself -- noticing your own thoughts, emotions, and actions. It's coming to understand that just as there is a part of you that can think, feel, or act a certain way, there is also a part of you that can observe your thoughts and behavior. For example, instead of feeling angry and not realizing it until it's too late, self-awareness helps you recognize and identify that you are starting to feel angry, in real time, while you still have a choice in how you respond. *Can you see the difference?* This made all the difference for me: going from being reactionary with my emotions to being proactive.

Through my practice of self-awareness, I have become an observer and student of myself and my own thoughts, feelings, and actions. With this kind of attention, I have come to a better understanding of myself and what makes me act the way I do.

Observing and understanding oneself isn't something we spend a lot of time doing, especially as parents. We have too much else to do. You may think to yourself, *Who has time for this any-*

way? Not me! I can barely find enough time to sleep! I get that but understand this: If you want to make a change, you will make time for this. The investment of becoming self-aware has paid huge dividends for me. Because of it, my parenting and my life are so much easier and less stressful now. So, read on.

Thank You Universe

Maybe the universe was trying to show me something. Perhaps it was just by chance. An unintended recording of myself gave me the opportunity to witness something I hadn't been able to see before.

I asked my son to put on shoes. We were trying to get out the door and we didn't have time to waste. I thought he was taking too long. He was unfocused and not really trying all that hard. At least, that's what I thought. I grew more and more impatient.

I wanted to leave and didn't want to spend another 10 minutes in the front hall watching him mess around.

Later, while walking down the street, I reached into my pocket, surprised to find the camera had been recording. I stopped the recording and listened to it. It was a huge wake-up call.

I had no idea I sounded like that. It was a bit shocking. I deleted it, embarrassed. My voice ranged from impatient, judgmental, and aggressive, to pleading, and then complaining -- all within about 90 seconds. I was all over the place, and decidedly negative.

My son was 4 at the time. I was 37.

A Big Dose of Self Awareness

This moment of truth affected me deeply. This inadvertent observation of myself gave me a big dose of self-awareness.

What am I teaching my son? What example am I setting? Is this kind of communication really going to motivate him? If I keep speaking to him like this, how will he see me? How will he see himself? What environment am I creating?

Observing myself allowed me to see my own behavior and evaluate it. The observation provided me with such useful information. After that day, I became more and more aware of my own behavior. This awareness greatly improved my parenting.

Being able to see oneself is an integral tool of improving performance across domains. Coaches film athletes and they review the videos together. Speakers, presenters, and performers do the same. In business and academia, feedback is part of the growth process. The best businesses invest in the development of their people and use constructive feedback frequently because they understand the importance of self-awareness.

The Real Teacher is Our Behavior

With a patient and positive kind of parenting, what we most need to master is our behavior... After all, we parent through behavior. We communicate through behavior. We teach through behavior. We model through behavior. We create relationships through behavior.

So much of parenting in the past has focused upon the child's behavior. Until that fateful moment, I had also focused on my child's behavior. Suddenly, however, I could clearly see that parenting is more about how **we** interact with our children than anything else. It is the moment-to-moment interactions and the tone they imbue, that weave together the tapestry of the home environment and the modeling our children receive.

Sometimes our behavior does not reflect the best of who we are. That's understandable. No one is perfect. However, with a vision and awareness of how we align with that vision, we can reset and repair. This allows us to model what to do when we make a mistake (apologize), and then to return to our intentions much more easily than if we had no vision at all and no awareness of ourselves.

Here is something you can ask yourself during your interactions with your child to bring more awareness to the situation:

What are my child's eyes seeing right now?

Exercise: Video Replay

Imagine watching a video of yourself during a challenging interaction with your child:

1. What do you see? Describe your behavior in terms of words spoken, tone of voice, facial expressions, and body language?

2. What do you understand about the parent in the video? How is that parent feeling?

3. What do you think your child is experiencing? Describe in detail.

4. What did you learn from this "video replay" exercise?

Emotions Drive Behavior

I spent the next few months observing my own behavior. I learned that my emotions preceded my behavior. If I felt angry, then there was a good chance that I would act in an angry way. Intellectually, I might have known this before, but observing this in real time, and in my life, gave me a much deeper understanding of this truth.

My behavior used to catch me off guard in the past. I remember not even realizing I was angry until after an outburst. I used to think that anger would sneak up on me, or that it came out of the blue. Now I know that this is not true. The emotions that led to my behavior didn't just come out of nowhere. They were always there, whether I was aware of them, or not. When emotions went unnoticed and unaddressed, they built up over time. With enough pressure, the anger volcano would erupt.

It is just plain hard to live in a world where you're unaware of your emotions, and the effect they have on you. It's confusing and disruptive. Without emotional intelligence, things feel out of control, unfair, and tiresome. In the years following my education in emotional intelligence, I have found that the words of Dr. John Gottman ring true:

"…science has discovered a tremendous amount about the role emotions play in our lives. Researchers have found that even more than IQ, your emotional awareness and abilities to handle feelings will determine your success and happiness in all walks of life…"

When I realized the true importance of knowing myself and understanding my emotions, I felt as if I had been admitted to a secret club. The secret club was that of **maturity**. You see, there are many people walking around in big bodies without big people maturity. Our emotions come out unpredictably, supercharged, and misdirected, because we were not taught how to identify and appropriately express our feelings. Perhaps they get stifled, suppressed, and avoided, until the volcano erupts again.

I wondered; how many other people knew about this? It didn't look like many. Seemingly, the world, our workplaces, our schools, and our families were largely unaware of this important truth. It seemed like most people, including me, could be caught off guard, confused and overwhelmed by their own emotions.

Questions:

1. *Were you taught how to feel your feelings when you were young? If not, what were you taught instead?*

2. *What benefits can you see from being able to identify and allow yourself to express your feelings?*

The Practice of Self-Awareness

The self-awareness exercise below helped me have more self-control and act more maturely, almost immediately. This exercise requires only a few quiet moments a day, and it's simple. You can do it on your own, at any time, and the more you do it, the better it works. It changed my life completely.

I became more skillful in *all* my relationships because I became more aware of the emotions that drove my behavior. I became familiar with my inner world and my behavior started to reflect what I actually wanted. Self-awareness allowed me to get off autopilot and start acting the way I intended.

Exercise: Self-Awareness

The point of this exercise is to slow down and observe yourself. It's a check-in that makes you aware of your personal emotional state in the moment. If you're not sure, you can start by describing what you are thinking; knowing your thoughts can help you uncover the underlying emotions.

Another way to start is by scanning the various areas of your life to see what comes up. How do you feel when you think about your spouse, children, work, health, or yourself?

Do some detective work and be curious. Also, be patient with yourself, as this exercise may be challenging the first few times you do it. Yes, it can be frustrating, but something is there, an identifiable emotion, and it will emerge if you give it some space and time.

You may find yourself having a hard time putting your finger on a specific emotion. That's okay. If you're like me, your emotional vocabulary might not be too extensive. I was not emotionally literate when I started this process, and I'm still learning.

For the first 35 years of my life, I think I used only two words to describe my emotional state: fine, and angry—and I'm pretty sure "fine" is not a real emotion. It was more like something I'd say during small talk. I have since expanded my emotional vocabulary and you can too. To get started in an easy way, use just 5 basic human emotions; mad, sad, glad, afraid, and ashamed. To take it further, look at the wheel of emotions that I mention below.

Once you identify an emotion, sit with it a moment to see if it feels accurate. If it doesn't quite fit, try something else on for size to get as close as you can to how you're feeling.

Do this exercise three times a day. After you learn to tune into yourself, all it takes is about two minutes in the morning, at midday, and in the evening to name the emotions you're experiencing.

That is 6 minutes or less a day.

Set an alarm on your phone with a reminder if that helps. Keep a journal and log the results. With such a small investment of time, there's no reason not to do this exercise. Do this exercise for a month and increase the frequency until you cultivate an ongoing awareness of the emotional state running in the background. The purpose is to bring your emotions out into the open. For me, this took a several weeks of constant checking in and journaling.

To be honest, I was not very good at this self-awareness practice at first. Sometimes, I'd tune in to myself and get nothing. Other times, I'd tune in to myself and get too much -- a confusing mess of thoughts and feelings. A part of me wondered if it was a waste of time.

Even though it was challenging and a part of me didn't like it, I stuck with it because *I needed to improve for my family*. I was out of options. A battle waged inside of me. One part of me thought, *This exercise is stupid, give it up.* Another part encouraged me to stick with it, knowing I was desperate to make a change for my kids. I can reassure you that if you persist, you *will* become aware of your current state, your thoughts, and your associated emotions. It will happen eventually.

With practice comes mastery, and there is no more important mastery than self-mastery.

Like I've said before, parenting is about the parent. We cannot be present and patient with our kids if we cannot do it for ourselves.

I will also warn you that it was uncomfortable to acknowledge and feel some of these feelings at first. I hadn't ever learned to do this. I had become accustomed to ignoring myself. Becoming conscious of my inner workings felt awkward and fumbly. I had done a fairly good job at convincing myself that I was "fine" over the course of my life and opening the door to some more vulnerable feelings was tough.

Sometimes this exercise had me questioning whether I was fine or not. That felt disconcerting. But now, I understand that it's impossible to be happy all the time. We are not robots, and yes, it's completely okay not to be happy, and to admit it. Hard to feel emotions are just as acceptable as lighter ones. Emotions are neither good nor bad.

Emotions provide us with useful information about ourselves that we can attend to. You're allowed to be sad, for example. Being sad, overwhelmed, or angry does not mean you're broken or weak, it means you're human. Welcome to your humanity.

If at any point you sense that your emotions are too big for you to handle, it's okay to get some help. There are professionals in this very field who are skilled at helping people make sense of and navigate big emotions. If this exercise or any other exercise in this book has you feeling big emotions that you don't know what to do with, please consider seeing a counselor or therapist.

Here are the supporting images/documents for the exercise. Go to my website and find the emotions log and wheel of emotions. https://drewtupper.com/emotion-log/.

Finally, here is the exercise:

1. Stop what you are doing. Find a comfortable position to sit or stand. Place your feet on the ground and take a few seconds to feel the connection to the earth. Close your eyes, take a deep breath, and notice that breath going into your body. Track the in and out. Bring attention to your body and to the inside of you. Let the breath infuse your whole body.
2. Get curious about how it feels to be in your body. Scan your body for any physical sensations you might be feeling. Scan your whole body from head to toe. Notice any physical sensations and just acknowledge them.
3. Pay attention to the general kind of feeling present in your body. Does it feel generally pleasant or not so pleasant to be in your body now? How much energy do you have? Now turn your attention to your emotional state. Name the emotion you're feeling. Notice the intensity of the emotion. Rate it on a scale of 1-10. For example: I am feeling Angry. It's a 6/10.

The idea is to become aware of yourself and your emotions, and to build a vocabulary around emotions. The aim of this exercise is just to notice, identify, and acknowledge your emotion without judgment.

In the next chapter, I talk about some strategies I used to regulate myself if I noticed a particularly challenging emotion present.

For now, when you feel challenging emotions, focus on identifying and accepting them. To do this, I use statements like these:

- "I can feel a tightness in my jaw."
- "I am feeling angry."
- "This is what is happening right now."
- "Even though I feel _____, I choose to accept myself"
- "It will eventually pass."

In short, I would detect a feeling in my body, nam the feeling, accept it, and allow it. When the feeling was challenging to feel. I would use the statements above. I would sit with it. Sometimes I would breathe into the feeling to help calm myself, but I will get more into that in the next chapter.

Coming Home to Your Body

Learning how to be self-aware was hard but it gave me the experience of feeling more connected to myself. I started to understand myself on a deeper level. I was able to listen to myself and had more compassion for myself. It felt like coming home.

I had the lived experience of really understanding that my emotions dictated my behavior. I also learned that my body could communicate with me. I could feel my emotions in my body.

These experiences showed me that the more aware I was of my emotions, the more control I had over myself. However, when I ignored my more challenging emotions, they had more control over my behavior.

Reducing the Power of Challenging Emotions

I noticed that the self-awareness exercise also had the power of diffusing the hard to feel emotions. Noticing myself and naming the difficult emotions brought them to light. "I see you anger/resentment, there you are. You are not so scary."

As an observer of myself, naming the emotion created space between me and the emotion. The grip of perceived negativity and reactivity loosened. Observation of my emotional state led me to see my emotions in a different way. I went from identifying with the emotion ("I am angry") to experiencing an emotion ("I am feeling angry"). This made a big difference.

Can you see how the power of a difficult emotion is immediately reduced by recognizing that it is something you're experiencing rather than something that you are? Awareness provides distance and healthy separation.

I came to understand that emotions come and go. When I stood back and noticed my emotions, I gained perspective. I understood that I was not the emotion itself, I was a person who was experiencing an emotion. With this ability to create space, my perspective shifted and my emotional maturity increased tenfold. I finally felt like I had found some hope.

When I recognized the emotion as temporary, it didn't feel so terminal and heavy. I learned that emotions move through us, they are not a life sentence.

Being an observer of myself *also* put me in more of a non-judgmental position. Before I learned to do this, not only would I feel bad, but I would feel bad about feeling bad. Labelling difficult emotions and accepting them put an end to that. Self-awareness plus self-acceptance is a strong medicine for the person who has been hard on themselves.

Understand this: It's okay to feel what you feel. It's okay to feel a full range of human emotions. Give yourself permission to feel. The more you allow yourself to feel challenging emotions, the less likely you are to act unconsciously from them.

Practice Self-Regulation

"You cannot manage what you are not aware of."
—Anonymous

After Awareness Comes Regulation

Self-regulation is the ability to control and direct oneself, especially in terms of one's values or long-term vision. Self-regulation is used by different people and organizations for a variety of purposes, but what I discuss here is *emotional* self-regulation.

Not surprisingly, the self-regulation that I needed to learn was what is called "down-regulation". Down-regulation helped me counter the effects of anxiety, anger, and stress. So, although self-regulation could mean to up-regulate from a less activated state to a more activated state, when I mention self-regulation, I am referring to calming, or down-regulation.

I started to see it like this: Self-awareness opens your eyes so that you see the messages your body is sending you. Self-awareness allows you to notice the warning signs your emotions are providing, and self-regulation allows you to choose the right path to handle them. Self-regulation gives you control over what you do with the emotions you're experiencing, as opposed to simply reacting to them -- often hurting those you love in the process. For example, just because I feel angry doesn't mean I have to express it in a hurtful way.

Together, self-awareness and self-regulation create the necessary space between stimulus and response that gives us a choice in our behavior. With choice comes control. With control comes more of being the parent you really want to be.

I found that if I don't practice awareness and regulation, my emotions go underground. They go *rogue*. If they go rogue, they bubble up and rise to the surface at unpredictable times and in uncontrollable ways. What could have been a slight annoyance or hiccup can turn into an anger volcano if compounded by other stressors and given enough time and pressure to build up. The exercises here allow you to relieve the pressure before it builds, then regroup, and refocus.

The mantras/affirmations that come to mind when I think about self-regulation are:

- I am 100 percent responsible for myself and my actions.
- I can feel my feelings, and then choose my behavior.
- My children learn from my example. My behavior is their biggest teacher.

Breathing is My Key to Self-Regulation

Conscious breathing is my basic unit of self-regulation. I came to see that when I can control my breath, I can control my behavior. And when I can control my behavior, I can control my life. It's as simple as that.

Below is a breathing exercise for you to do in conjunction with the "Emotional State Check-In Exercise" from the previous chapter. Do the check-in first and then do this breathing exercise right after to help regulate yourself.

Also, I invite you to use this breathing exercise outside of the scheduled times. Use this kind of breathing whenever you feel yourself getting emotionally dysregulated. I even use it when I'm having a hard time sleeping at night.

Exercise: Breathing to Regulate

1. Plant your feet on the ground. Close your eyes. Place one hand on your heart and the other on your abdomen or find a different hand placement that works for you.
2. Breathe in a big deep belly (diaphragmatic) breath. Breathe in for a count of 5 seconds. Send the breath all the way down into your belly. The belly must expand on the in-breath and contract on the out-breath. This is the reverse to how most people breathe. At the top of the in-breath, when your belly is full of air, pause. Hold that for a count of 3 seconds.
3. Let your breath out slowly. Make the exhale twice as long as the inhale (10 seconds). Make a sound when you breathe out, like an "ahhh" or "haaa" sound. The idea is to let the breath come out super slowly and controlled. To get the idea, imagine you are trying to fog up a mirror. If you know yoga, you can restrict the throat like Ujjayi breath on the inhale and exhale. Hold your breath for 3 seconds at the bottom of the breath.

Repeat the cycle 5 times.

Here are some more nuances on how I do the breathing. I breathe into where I feel tension. I imagine that when I breathe, I am breathing in expansion, relaxation, and even love into the areas that are holding tension and stress. When I breathe out, I let out the tension I feel there. Places where I usually hold tension are my chest, my jaw, my eyes, and my hands. When I do this exercise, I pay attention to these areas. I relax my jaw, I soften my eyes, and shake out my hands. I invite openness, expansion, and relaxation into the parts of my body where I feel tense and constricted.

When I finish the breathing exercise, I slow down my talking, so that I can still do a few bigger and slower breaths in between sentences. With the help of the breath, you should be able to switch to a gentler, slower, and more encouraging way of talking. This will calm you even more. Consider putting on a gentle smile, not a big fake Ronald McDonald smile, but an ever-so-gentle smile. Soften your eyes and forehead. This will have you feeling even more relaxed.

This exercise takes advantage of the fact that your physiology affects your thinking, your emotions, and your behaviors. It is a neat trick. We usually think of the mind controlling the body. However, when you adjust your physiology to reflect that of a calm state, your nervous system sends messages to your brain to calm down.

You can breathe yourself out of a stressed state.

Self-Check-In Time

1. How did you feel after doing the deep belly breaths?

2. What did you notice about your body and your thinking?

3. If this felt calming for you, what do you think would happen if you breathed like this when you were feeling angry/tense/reactive?

For me, I have noticed that although this breath work does not take long, it has a profoundly calming effect on my internal state. In the beginning, I needed to do more than 5 cycles, sometimes 10 or 20, depending on my state. For some, I understand this breathing exercise might not feel good. If this does not feel good for you, I mention some other things that you can try below in #3 of **Exercising Choice**. For some people, it is possible that calming exercises can induce more stress, even panic. If this is you, please consider seeking out professional help. Somatic Experiencing professionals work with the body and nervous system in very effective ways to promote self-regulation, even in cases of significant trauma.

Your Self-Regulation Leads to Your Child's Self-Regulation

If you need space or privacy to do this, go ahead; however, I encourage you to think about eventually normalizing the practice. As strange as it might feel, if your children see you doing this, they'll likely start doing it, too. Remember, we teach by example. And apparently, we feel by example too.

There is something called emotional contagion that is based on mirror neurons in the brain. The emotional contagion phenomenon results in one person's emotions and related behaviors triggering similar emotions and behaviors in another person. (_Hatfield, Elaine; Cacioppo, John T.; Rapson, Richard L: in Wikipedia_)

For parents, this is good news. We can take advantage of brain physiology to infuse feelings of calm into the environment and in our children by _demonstrating what_ calm looks like ourselves. This is especially important as children need help with this. Children are not born with the capacity to down regulate all that well. It must be developed. Children learn how to self-regulate by _co-regulating_ first, with a caregiver who models the behavior.

Be careful though. Emotional contagion can work in reverse. If the caregiver is not aware of, and able to regulate, his/her own emotions, an upset or anxious child can trigger an upset or anxious state. Being aware of this, we can choose to be the one transmitting calm to the child, especially when they are upset, and they need our guidance. I have found that this is best done when my children see my calm face, hear me talking calmly, and see me breathing calmly. Essentially, I overtly embody the calm I wish to see.

What do you think would happen if your children learned that they could do something to help themselves when they get dysregulated? Imagine if you had learned a simple self-regulation tool, like intentional breathing, when you were young. How do you think that would have helped you throughout your life?

I have found that no exercise cures me of anger or reactivity. It's not that you won't ever be angry again, but practicing awareness allows you to catch yourself so much sooner than you would have before. These exercises calm you down so that you can redirect yourself to choose a more productive response.

Acting toward what you want is one of the most powerful and uplifting things you can do for yourself. You come to know that you are an active agent in creating how you think, behave, and feel. You get to experience that you have the power and capability to make things better. You prove to yourself that you can respond, instead of reacting. *You are not a receiver of circumstances; you are a creator of situations.* You get to watch yourself turn off autopilot and chart your own course. I used to think things were hopeless and that I was destined to press on with my reactive ways. But that wasn't true for me, and it need not be true for you. Improvement is totally possible, inevitable even, when you use these simple tools.

Exercise: Understanding and Helping Yourself

After feeling a challenging emotion, ask yourself these things:

1. *Why did/do I feel like this?*

After fully accepting how I feel, I get curious about *why* I'm feeling the way I am. The act of being curious leads you down a much more productive path than self-recrimination, judgment, and shame.

For me, tracing the cause of the emotions I was experiencing reduced the power challenging emotions had over me. It solidified my observer position even more. I would think: *this emotion is only something I am experiencing.* Curiosity created space. It inserted another buffer between my emotions and actions. Also, I realized that if I was busy being curious about how I felt, then at least I wasn't simply acting on it.

Tracing back where things went off track helped me inhabit more of a problem-solving mindset. It felt empowering and compassionate for me to really try to understand myself. Asking the *Why do I feel like this?* question acknowledges there was a reasonable explanation for how I felt. It felt good to understand that there was a reason, and that it could be understood and even addressed.

2. *Do I want to shift how I feel?*

This question demonstrates that you are not captive to your emotions—you have a choice. Becoming aware of your underlying state allows you to choose if you want to continue putting energy toward feeling how you are feeling. Can you imagine getting to choose how you want to feel?

For me, realizing that I had agency in where and how I spent my energy was liberating.

3. What (else) do I need? /What can I do to help myself?

Do you need something other than the breathing exercise to help you feel even more balanced? Maybe. I often did, especially when this was new to me, or when I was particularly agitated. Asking yourself what else you need, and then taking action accomplishes a couple good things: 1. It further interrupts the cycle you are in. It takes away momentum from an unwanted behavior pattern and puts the momentum toward something more constructive. 2. It is also self-compassionate. Because self-judgment is a major reason why a lot of people are angry and frustrated. Compassion is a key countermeasure to judgement and anger.

Here are a few things I do to shift my state to a more balanced calm:

- Take space, take a walk, and do more belly breathing
- Talk to a caring and good listener about how I feel, or journal how I feel, where I feel it, and what that feeling feels like in my body.
- Exercise, meditate, do yoga, shake my body.
- Express any anger physically in a safe way: Yell into a pillow. Punch a pillow. Scream in my car.

These types of activities can be used to help you further calm down. I also use them preemptively on a regular basis to form part of a self-care routine that curbs acts of anger before they even happen. And even though most of my regulation was to down regulate myself, I noticed that some of these strategies were also effective the few times I wanted to upregulate myself.

Questions:

1. Can you think of other ways to help yourself calm down if you become stressed, reactive, or angry?

2. Think back to a time when you became angry or reactive. What do you think led to it? What could you have done before becoming angry to shift how you felt? What did you need, or what could you have done for yourself?

A Warning

Your programming will try hard to pull you back. Feeling calm might not feel all that familiar. Humans are creatures of habit. If you have been tightly wound and reactive for a long time, that's likely what is going to feel familiar. Those tracks are well worn. The body likes familiar. There is a learning curve to this.

Don't expect to be Mary Poppins on day 1. Setting expectations too high diminished my morale and plunged me back into the self-judgement/anger vortex. I came to understand that I had some work to do, and it wasn't going to happen overnight. I also realized that if there was just *one moment in one day* where I chose something different, I could consider that a win. Harm reduction was the name of the game at the beginning of my journey. I decided to take the little wins.

I remember feeling awkward when I first started to get control of myself. It almost felt like sticking a wrench into the gears of a machine. The gears were strong and wanted to keep turning. It seemed as if my body was conditioned to continue in an angry way.

For example, the first time I managed to get control of myself amid climbing Anger Mountain, I noticed some things: I had a tight feeling in my chest and my head felt hot. *Oh,* I thought. *I have felt this before. I know what this is. It's anger.*

I was present to the anger in the moment and thought, *If I continue like this, I'm going to blow up on someone, probably my son.*

I don't want to do that. I am going to remove myself from the situation. It was surreal. I had successfully stopped the train from chugging up Anger Mountain. Wow, it felt powerful to have so much control over myself. I felt a bit like Yoda.

What followed perplexed me, though. Not long after, I had an urge to continue chugging up the mountain. The autopilot was strong within me. A battle was waging. On one hand, the newly aware part of me said, *You don't want to go there. You've done this before. It doesn't work well, you know that. Choose something different here. Being aggressive, yelling, and blaming are not the way. You know this. You can choose something better.* The other voice said, *You can't just sit there and do nothing. He is being disrespectful. He needs to listen. You need to make him listen. You can't let him get away with this.*

This is what I want to call attention to. When you act in a new way that is less punitive and less harmful, it might feel "incomplete" and unsatisfying at first. It might feel like you haven't done your job, or like your child is getting away with something; it may feel like the train needs to stay on its angry reactive course.

Personally, I hoped that doing the right thing would feel more gratifying. But I was left wanting more. Don't let this fool you. This is not your best self speaking. This is likely not your values asserting themselves. This is your ego and its programming. It's a sign that programming runs deep.

There is an addictive quality to lashing out. There is a hit or a rush one gets from losing control. In this way, there is a pull to continue behaviors that are not helpful. Changing my parenting behavior was hard, and it continues to be so. That's the truth of it. I want to mention this in case parents imagine that because it doesn't *feel* good that it must not *be* good. The journey is not necessarily an easy journey, but it is a journey worth staying on.

You will feel frustrated but stay the course. Changing negative programming and breaking hurtful habits is important, so don't give up on doing the right thing. Parenting is a long game. Remember you're doing this for other reasons than a quick fix or what feels good in the moment.

I encourage you to trade in your impulsivity and anger for something that is going to be better for you and your kids: mature loving leadership. I encourage you to be the author of the most loving and inspiring story you can. Your children need you to do so.

Practice Self-Care

"Your relationship with yourself sets the tone
for every other relationship you have."
—Robert Holden

Self-Care is Not Just Spa Days

Persistent high levels of stress are counter-productive to being emotionally intelligent. There is a long list of negative impacts that prolonged elevated stress levels can have on one's body and mind. From the standpoint of emotional intelligence, stress negatively affects our ability to remain calm, connected, and in control.

An article written by Dr. Mills et. al. (2008) outlined the many ways that high stress levels can negatively impact our ability to be self-aware and self-regulated. Below are some of the personality changes witnessed in people when highly stressed:

- Irritability
- Hostility
- Frustration
- Anger
- Aggressive feelings and behavior
- Excessive defensiveness or suspiciousness

- Problems in communication
- Social withdrawal and isolation
- Impulsivity

Managing stress was a big part of managing myself and my behavior; I noticed first-hand that having high and persistent levels of stress made it difficult to act like the parent and person I wanted to be.

Even with new goals and new strategies, enough stress could slingshot me back to reactive and harmful behaviors that I didn't want to engage in. I found that the higher the stress running in the background of my life, the more likely it was that I'd get triggered or have an outburst.

Looking back, it's like I was constantly riding close to the edge, and it didn't take much to push me over. I wasn't setting myself up for success. In this way, I understood that managing the overall level of stress in my life was important for the success of my parenting. Persistent stress changed my personality, making me high-strung and reactive. I also noticed that the outlet for my stress was often my children. This was not fair to them, and they didn't deserve it.

To address the negative effects of stress on my life and my parenting, I had to take a more global or "zoomed out" view of my life. I had to ask some important questions, ones which I invite you to ask yourself:

Questions:

1. How do high levels of stress affect your behavior?

2. How does your stress affect your children's behavior?

3. How does your lifestyle contribute to higher levels of stress?

What is Self-Care?

Self-care is made up of intentional activities used to combat the negative effects of stress. Self-care helps to restore and rejuvenate one's mental, emotional, spiritual, and physical health. The concept seems simple, but it's often overlooked, not taken seriously, or worse, dismissed as "indulgent". If you were not taught how to do this, you may not even know about it. I was aware of restorative activities, but I wasn't aware of the real importance of them or the need to schedule such activities until I committed to walking a kinder and more loving path overall.

Self-care can be difficult for busy parents, but as the saying on airplanes goes, you must put on your own oxygen mask first before you help others. I noticed first-hand that I was not much help to others, nor was I a good role model, when I was stressed and angry.

I was a much better parent after taking care of myself in some way. My reactions were less hasty, and I had more patience with my kids. I've learned that I must make myself a priority so that I can remain patient and calm.

Practicing self-care can get misconstrued for being selfish. Self-care is not something to feel bad or guilty about. It's a necessary part of being healthy. We cannot consistently give our kids our best if we are not feeling resourced.

Each self-care regimen will look different, but ultimately, self-care should be stress-reducing and restorative. It should fill you up, not drain you. My self-care list has changed over the years, but has included the following at different times:

- Maintaining social supports and regularly expressing my emotions to people who I trust and who can witness me without judgment

- Breathing exercises
- Practicing gratitude
- Saying no to things that drain me
- Spending time being active in nature (hiking, rock climbing, surfing)
- Exercising or playing sports regularly
- Maintaining good nutrition with special attention to reducing caffeine, alcohol, and sugar
- Getting 7+ hours of good sleep a night
- Seeing a counselor
- Maintaining a meditation practice
- Cuddling with loved ones or animals
- Listening to or making music and/or dancing
- Playing/making time for being silly and playing games
- Being creative (painting, woodworking, gardening, building)
- Writing
- Watching comedies
- Having a hot/cold tub, bath, or shower
- Doing work that matters
- Living my values (taking responsibility for my actions)
- Focusing on solutions rather than ruminating on problems
- Delegating tasks and sharing the workload

Start Small, Get Easy Wins

Different people will need different things. Do what works for you. When you engage in self-care, you're taking pre-emptive steps towards lowering your stress and improving your mood.

The key to truly accomplishing self-care is to *schedule it* into your calendar, then actually do it. To make things easy, start small. Self-care isn't all about grand gestures, anyway. Taking small breaks throughout the day adds up, especially if your work is demanding. When I had young kids and felt busy, if I didn't do anything else, I made sure that I was doing the belly breathing exercise three times a day. The difference between doing and not doing just that one thing was very noticeable.

Another trick is to combine two or three of these at one time, a technique called habit-stacking. What could you stack together to make your self-care more efficient and enjoyable? Perhaps you could go on a walk each evening, do some breathing, sit on a park bench, and then write an entry in your gratitude journal. Doing this accomplishes three things at the same time.

Questions:

1. What is your history with self-care? How well-rested and well-resourced do you regularly feel?

2. Do you currently have a self-care regimen? What do you do to effectively manage or reduce your levels of stress?

Tightly Wound People

I've noticed that different people will have different levels of underlying stress and will require different strategies and different amounts of intervention to regulate. For example, my nervous system was tightly wound, and I tended to be generally anxious. I found that self-care was particularly important for me. How do you know if you are tightly wound? For me, it expressed itself like this. I was:

- Vigilant, looking for danger
- Very protective of children
- Controlling
- Emotionally reactive
- Fast-moving
- Fast-talking

- High-pitched talking at times
- Poor sleep at times

It's funny; I wouldn't have said I was stressed or anxious. I thought it was normal to be acting the way I was. I also wouldn't have wanted to admit that I was anxious. I would have seen it as a weakness. My outward appearance was fun and easygoing, or at least I thought it was. Being honest about this was hard for me but lowering my underlying level of stress has helped me gain more self-control.

Question:

What is your underlying level of stress? Do you think you might be tightly wound or anxious?

Self care is an extremely important tool for those who tend toward being tightly wound or anxious. If you are still having a hard time dealing with your levels of stress and anxiety after reading this book and implementing changes, consider reaching out for some professional help.

In the previous chapter, we talked about self-regulation tools that can be used to help you in challenging moments when stress or difficult emotions arise. Self-care is different because it allows you to reduce your overall stress levels. Self-care does not replace the awareness and regulation work that we've already talked about, it adds to it. With self-awareness, self-regulation, and self-care under your belt, you're well on your way to being a calm, mature, and emotionally intelligent person, and parent.

Valuing Yourself

Self-care is essential to a good relationship with yourself. I started showing myself love by making myself a priority. Engaging in self-care was like sending the message to myself that I was important and worth my own time and attention. Not only did self-care help reduce my stress and increase my patience, it increased my self-esteem and confidence as well.

That was a powerful combination: to feel more in control *and* feel better about myself. Again, I felt like I had been given access to a secret club. I looked around at other people practicing self-care and noticed something -- they seemed more in control of themselves as well, they appeared to like themselves better, and they were happier in general. There truly is some magic that happens when you make yourself a priority and engage in life-giving and restorative activities. All aspects of the self benefit: the mental, physical, emotional, and spiritual.

Why Self-Care Can Be Hard

Like any habit you're trying to form, self-care requires discipline. There are logistics to sort out. Arrangements need to be made. New habits are not always easy to acquire. For the mechanics behind building successful habits, I'd refer you to the book *Atomic Habits* by James Clear.

Here, I will address some of the beliefs that got in the way of me taking time for myself. Maybe you'll be able to relate.

First off, maintaining a self-care regimen was hard for me because I felt the need to be there for my family. That's the story that I told myself—a good parent is always present and sacrifices his time. There is some truth here. There are sacrifices to be made.

However, there's a point when sensible sacrifice crosses over to depriving yourself, resulting in exhaustion and resentment. Playing the martyr was not restorative and not in the best interest of my family. It left me feeling even more anxious and unappreciated. Looking for appreciation from others to help you feel better is a dangerous game to play. You give your power away by relying on others to make you feel good, instead of relying on yourself.

I found that the appreciation that I was looking for was my own. Self-appreciation is far more reliable anyway, and more meaningful as well. Self-care was the most tangible way I could demonstrate to myself that I appreciated—and even loved—myself.

Another reason self-care was hard for me was because I had a hard time delegating. Honestly, I had a hard time asking others for help and trusting that they could do the job as well as I could.

With anxiety and control issues, it was very hard to ask for help and trust others. It was a leap of faith for me to let go of control.

Excuses popped up as they often do: "I don't have time," "I can't find childcare," "I can't afford it," "I don't feel like it." All these excuses can be addressed if your motivation is strong enough and parenting better was a very strong motivator for me.

However, it wasn't always easy to stick with it. It took more than a couple of relapses into my controlling martyrdom for me to understand the importance of self-care. Because I was now able to observe myself, I saw what I was like when I engaged in self-care versus when I didn't.

The evidence was overwhelming. I decided that self-care wasn't luxury, it was a necessity. I was stressed, edgy, and down when I didn't take care of myself. The opposite was true when I made myself a priority and showed myself some love. Simply put, I was a much better parent when I practiced self-care.

Exercise: The Energy Audit

Make a list with two columns. On one side, write down the activities that are calming, life-giving, or restorative, whether you do them or not. Use your imagination and my self-care list above for inspiration if needed.

On the other side, list the activities you do that are stressful or life-draining. Be mindful of even small activities and expenditure of energy. The trick is to scan your whole day, even your whole life, and to be as honest as possible with yourself.

Looking at your list, what life-giving activities can you say yes to and incorporate into your life? These can be activities done throughout the day, like mini-meditations, or weekly scheduled activities like yoga. What about the draining activities? What can you say no to or reduce?

Schedule the changes on your calendar. If time is an issue, be creative and look for down time or moments where you might not be spending time wisely. For many people there is an opportunity to get up earlier, or to replace some screen time with more restorative activities. Start small and stay consistent. Do this activity with a partner or friend to add a level of accountability.

Live in Integrity

"The wind might cause a kite to rise, but what keeps it up there is the fact that somebody on the ground has a steady hand. You have to hold steady to your values - your integrity. It's your anchor. You let go of that…well, it isn't long before your kite comes crashing down."
—Mark Victor Hansen and Robert G. Allen

Integrity a.k.a. Living Your Values

I feel best when I act in alignment with my values. In fact, the more I live my values, the more centered, purposeful, and at peace I feel. The more I live my values, the better I sleep at night. When I act in ways that are out of alignment with my values, I simply don't feel good.

Few people are aware that being out of integrity with one's values is a major cause of stress. What's happening, as far as I can tell, is this: when we aren't who we want to be, we get upset with ourselves. When we ignore our values, the disappointment we experience goes deep to our core and causes resentment and anxiety.

For example, there were times at work, or with friends and family members that I agreed to things I didn't want to do. Instead of being honest, respecting my own autonomy, and asserting my desires, I betrayed myself by pretending that things were ok with me when they weren't. Honesty and autonomy are important values to me. So, this behavior of mine was counter to my own values, both at the moment of agreement, and then again in the doing of it.

Agreeing to do something I didn't want to do was a way to keep the peace, at least I thought. However, it was an abandoning of myself and my values. So, what was truly happening, is that while I was keeping the peace outside, I was destroying the peace inside. Abandoning my values in this way caused a resentment of myself that was toxic to me and to my relationships. Being upset with myself was counterproductive to being a good parent for my children. I ended up taking the resentment and resulting frustration from not living my values out on the people closest to me. Unfortunately, this is what many parents do. This is a hard one to see, but I'm telling you, it is there if you are brave enough to look.

Questions:

1. Do you live by a code of values? If so, what are your values?

2. Recall times in your life when you abandoned your values. What did it feel like and what happened?

3. Think of a time when you lived your values, even though it may have been difficult to do so. What did it feel like and what happened?

Exercise: Identifying Your Values

Looking In

> Think about memorable times in your life when you were the most satisfied and deeply fulfilled. What was happening in those moments? Can you see the values that influenced those moments?

Looking Out

> What kind of people do you admire and respect? Who inspires you, and why? What do they do differently than others? Can you see any values in those people that you appreciate and would like to live by?

Identify Your Most Important Values

What values are represented when you look in and look out? Scrutinize these memories, experiences, and people. Use the list below, if needed, to crystallize your understanding of exactly what your values are. Identify your top six values based on your answers in the exercise. What values are present in these memories and in these people?

Take your time. Dig deeply to find out why you appreciate these things so much.

Authenticity	Friendship	Peace
Adventure	Freedom	Pleasure
Authority	Fun	Popularity
Autonomy	Growth	Purpose
Assertive	Happiness	Recognition
Balance	Honesty	Reputation
Beauty	Humor	Respect
Bravery	Inner Harmony	Responsibility
Compassion	Justice	Security
Challenge	Kindness	Self-Respect
Community	Knowledge	Service
Competency	Leadership	Spirituality
Contribution	Learning	Stability
Creativity	Love	Success
Curiosity	Loyalty	Status
Determination	Meaningful Work	Trustworthiness
Fairness	Openness	Wealth
Faith	Optimism	Wisdom

Look at your list of six values and ask yourself, *If I could only satisfy three of these, which ones would I choose?* The reason for doing this is similar to prioritizing what you would want to accomplish by the time your children leave the home. Life is busy, so you only have a certain amount of bandwidth. Prioritizing my values has helped me greatly. I use them as a touchstone to live my life. I ask myself again and again how I can bring my values into each situation I encounter. Continue doing this until it becomes automatic. Now, when I slip out of integrity, I can feel it right away and I can do something about it. My internal compass keeps me from getting lost.

The Internal Compass

The emotional intelligence work I did clued me into feelings of resentment and frustration when I abandoned my values. It also clued me into feelings of resonance or purpose when I was in integrity. In a way, I was able to *feel* when I was living my values. The awareness and regulation work we've covered allows you to know your values and to actively choose to live them each day. It's a skill to know who you are, what your values are, and then to embody that day in, day out. Being in integrity isn't always easy, but the inner peace it brings to an individual cannot be overestimated.

I believe that living one's values is the most powerful and sustainable way to happiness and fulfillment. The more I doubled down on living my values, the more purposeful and peaceful I felt. I also noticed that the more I lived my values, the less I felt the need to numb the pain of not living in alignment. I noticed I didn't drink as much and didn't eat as much unhealthy food. I also didn't watch as much TV and didn't feel the need for much distraction or mindless entertainment in my life. I think that is because living one's values is exciting. It's edgy and risky at times. Telling the truth about who you are and then living that truth is exhilarating. No need for numbing or substitutes when you have the real thing.

Reaffirm Your Top Values

Reaffirm your list by asking yourself:

- Do these values make me feel good about myself?
- Would I feel comfortable telling people about them?
- Would I live these values, even if it was hard to do so?
- Do these values fit for me and the vision of my family I created?

Living my values is not just about reacting to situations in a way that's consistent to the values. Though this is great to do, there is more to it. Living my values means going out in the world, being proactive, and creating situations and moments that are infused with the values close to my heart. I have found that living one's values is an active process that requires courage and consistency.

Questions

1. After reflecting on your values, what is one thing you could do to live more in alignment with your values and how exactly will you do that?

2. How will you stay accountable to living your values?

3. What happens if you choose not to pay attention to the importance of living your values?

Living is Teaching

Children learn values from watching our behavior, not from us telling them what values they should adopt. The values you hold close and make a priority are going to be noticed by your children as you demonstrate them day in and day out. Values are not taught but caught. If you want to impart the power of living certain values, first and foremost, you're going to have to live those values yourself. We cannot claim honesty as a value and have our children witness us telling little lies. We cannot claim respect as a value and then disrespect our children. We cannot claim generosity as a value and then live a self-centered life. Again, the parent's behavior is the real teacher.

Exercise: Values Check-In

Add a Values check-in to the emotional state check in. Three times a day, stop to ask yourself the following question: *Am I living my values?"*

We Reap What We Sow

The world wants a full expression of you, and you want this, too. The human heart yearns to live fully expressed and in alignment with its internal compass. I have felt this pull, and I have felt the magic of stepping into a life of taking the risk of living my values. I don't always succeed, but when I do, there seems to be a different quality and resonance in my life.

Imagine what would be possible if we all stepped forward and decided to live the best of who we are, day in and day out, for ourselves and for our children. Imagine what would be possible for our children and our communities.

It's your choice but know this: there is no real escape. *Either you strive to live your values or deal with the life you create when you don't.* It's a tough realization to come to, but it's also the path to freedom.

Understand the Child

"Understanding physics is child's play when
compared to understanding child's play."
—Albert Einstein

Perception is Everything

Perception is a powerful thing. Thoughts and beliefs create our reality. If we *believe* something is good, we tend to *experience* it as good and look for ways to confirm that it is good.

The opposite is true—if we believe something to be bad or flawed, we will experience it as such and look for ways to confirm that negative perception. For example, you can perceive a child as manipulating you to get attention, or alternatively, looking to connect and feel loved, seen, and heard. Similarly, you can perceive a child as being disobedient and disrespectful or as being curious and lacking self-control.

These days, I *choose* to see the positive, but it wasn't always that way. In the past, I thought that children were manipulative troublemakers. I thought that my children were trying to make things hard for me. And, predictably, I ended up seeing what I expected to see. I saw my children as disrespectful, entitled, and lazy. The labels *I* created influenced how I saw my children. I confirmed my own bias again and again. This is how powerful perception is. It can shape your own reality and the reality of the children you parent.

It became clear that how I saw my world influenced my world. How I saw my children influenced how I interacted with them. When I saw my children as good and well-meaning, my tone, my body language, and my words reflected that. Unfortunately, the opposite was also true.

When you believe someone to be fundamentally good, you end up seeing the best in them and speaking to the best in them. A child who is treated and spoken to as if he is good will believe he is good, will feel good, and will look for ways to express goodness. A child who is continually judged and labeled may just eventually live into those labels like a self-fulfilling prophecy.

A big part of understanding my children has come down to seeing them not just as kids, but as humans. I've learned to treat my children as I would want to be treated.

Questions:

1. In your heart, how do you view your children? Deep down, who do you believe them to be? Is how you treat them consistent with how you see them?

2. How would they think you view them? You could try asking them but be prepared to listen openly.

3. How do you feel when someone assumes the best of you, believes in you, and treats you as such? What about the opposite?

Good Kids, but Not Easy

After I made a choice to see my children as inherently good, it took discipline to choose that perspective when things got challenging. Precisely because they are children, children often lack the self-awareness, self-control, and skills to understand and express themselves articulately when they get upset. Honestly, it can get a bit ugly. This was hard to deal with and it really challenged my belief that they were good. So many times, I was tempted to throw in the towel and let their behavior "confirm" my judgmental beliefs about them.

Kids will use their voice and body to communicate feeling upset. They will yell, whine, stomp, hit, run away, or shut down. This can feel annoying, upsetting, and frustrating. If that's not enough, children lack perspective that their behavior impacting anyone else. We then interpret this as the child being self-centered and unappreciative.

However, this lack of awareness makes sense from a brain development perspective. The prefrontal cortex does not fully develop for humans until they're in their mid 20s.

According to GoodTherapy.com, the prefrontal cortex contributes to a wide variety of executive functions, including:

- Focusing one's attention
- Predicting the consequences of one's actions; anticipating events in the environment
- Impulse control; managing emotional reactions
- Planning for the future
- Coordinating and adjusting complex behaviors ("I can't do A until B happens")

(Source: https://www.goodtherapy.org/blog/psychpedia/prefrontal-cortex)

Children are Still Developing, Learning, and Maturing

Children do not have full capacity for self-control and impulse control like mature adults do. We cannot judge them by the standards we would for a full-grown adult. The world that children are living in can be quite confusing to them, frustrating, and full of big emotions that they are not equipped to handle yet. They need our guidance and patience to help them learn how to navigate their world. This is what parenting is.

Because their sense of self-control and awareness of others is still developing, they will make mistakes and engage in some dysregulated and undesirable behaviors that can feel to us like disrespect and manipulation. Our job is to regulate ourselves, love them through this and help them grow.

Developmentally, this all makes sense, but it doesn't mean it's easy to deal with. I regularly have a hard time finding patience. This is why I repeatedly tell myself they are good and still developing. Combining this shift in perspective with my own self-regulation and self-care skills helped me stay centered and focused on how I wanted to parent, even when things got tough.

In other words, the skills, and abilities we often blame children for not having are the very things we need to teach them and help them develop. It's unreasonable for us to expect that the perspective and skills I'm teaching you in this book should be innate in our children. And remember, we teach by modeling.

Have hope. I have seen my children learn how to self-regulate and communicate in more mature ways as they grow, especially as my approach shifted to having more patience with them and as I modeled healthier and more loving kinds of behavior.

I now know that my children were never trying to make my life hard, as much as they were having a hard time. Replacing the idea

84

that my children were disrespectful with the idea that my child needed help and guidance was a very helpful shift to make. It allowed me to not take things so personally, and at the same time, it helped me feel like a leader with an important purpose. My purpose was to rise to the challenge and help them in difficult moments, to help them build skills and to do it all with my mature and loving presence.

Understanding Misbehavior

If I take the leap of faith that my child is good and wants to do well, then everything gets filtered through that lens. All "bad" behavior is seen as either a skill that has not been acquired or an honest mistake. If I assume my child to be good, then everything he does that looks contrary to that is taken as a misstep and/or an opportunity to learn. It is never personal. There is no malevolence.

My job then becomes to help my child figure out what is going on. I have discovered there's often a need driving the behavior. I firmly believe that every need can be met in a reasonable, pro-social way. Think about their need for attention, for example. Children will try to meet this need in any way they can. I believe when children can't meet their needs in positive ways, they communicate this frustration in a negative way. That's how strong the need is. It's central to who they are and therefore cannot be dismissed or diminished. So, now I often think to myself: *if their current behavior is not working, how can I help?*

Questions:

1. Do you find it difficult to understand or remember that your children are good at heart? What gets in the way of you understanding this? Do you have a hard time remembering you are good at heart?

2. Do you have any negative labels for your children? How could you reword these labels to see the best in your child? For example: *attention-seeking* could be reworded to *connection-seeking*.

Children Are Just Like Us

Children are trying to get by and navigate life just like the rest of us. In fact, I find children to be innocent and straight-forward. They have no hidden agenda. They are good-natured and just want to be happy. I came to this conclusion after years of observation and interaction with children. It's just true.

What I saw again and again was children simply trying to be children. I saw children wanting to play, learn, express themselves, feel safe, feel loved, feel engaged and valued. That's it. These were the motivating factors behind the behaviors I saw. So much of the behavior I witnessed was geared towards getting those needs met, or, on the other hand, protesting the fact that these needs weren't being met. That's it. It kind of shocked me how simple it was.

This is the general pattern I observed: when children got their needs met, they seemed to be happy and cooperative. When they couldn't get their needs met, they felt upset and would protest with uncooperative behavior. This is how important these needs are to kids. It was a simple, but profound, realization.

These needs of children are not unreasonable. They make sense, and because need seems to be so closely related to behavior/misbehavior, they are worth understanding. The secret seemed to be that if I could help my children *feel* good, then they would *do* good—not just for me, but because they felt secure, connected, and happy. This made sense and was consistent with an earlier observation I made of myself: my behavior was largely dictated by my emotions. If deep down I felt good, safe, secure, and loved, then my behavior reflected it. If this made sense for me then why would it not be the same for children?

Rebranding Misbehavior

After seeing how my emotions could so strongly impact my own behavior, I started to see how this would be true for my kids, too. And if behavior was an indication of how someone felt, then the following must be true, too: A child not behaving well must not be feeling good. As a result, misbehavior could be seen as a child's way of broadcasting her upset or frustration.

It could also be seen as a call for help. In this regard, replacing punishment or consequences with curiosity and a desire to help has completely changed the game for me. I have become better at detecting what emotion is driving my children's behavior and, therefore, what their unmet needs are. I am then able to help them meet that need. The results have been impressive. When I focus on helping, I can de-escalate and resolve situations in a way that allows everyone to retain dignity and connection. That's a big deal, and much better than resolving situations through negativity, fear, or coercion that leads to shame and disconnection.

Understanding my children's needs and collaborating with them to meet those needs has allowed me to use the time and energy that I used to use coaxing and waging power struggles on more important things. Understanding my children has allowed me to get to the root of issues and find sustainable solutions, rather than simply applying Band-Aids that don't address the source of the wound. Understanding my children has allowed me to effectively empower them to express themselves, advocate for themselves, and to take responsibility for themselves. Where we used to find lots of problems, we now find many creative solutions.

This shift in perspective propelled us from simply surviving to thriving. My children responded very well. They seemed to understand that I was genuinely trying to help them and not just control them. I trusted them and they began to trust me and relax into me. Our relationship—and their behavior—improved. This is when I started to feel like a skillful parent and leader, like I catching on to how good and mature parenting worked.

Exercise: Hindsight is Often 20-20

Think back to a time when you thought your child was misbehaving. Can you imagine how their misbehavior could have been tied to a feeling he or she was experiencing, or a need that was not being met? How so?

What Exactly are "Needs"?

I already knew that I was supposed to pay attention to the physical needs of my child: hunger, sleep, physical activity, pees, and poops. What escaped my realm of consciousness were the less than obvious, more emotional, or psychological needs that were important to my children.

Through observation, I noticed needs that appeared to be important to the well-being and the prosocial behavior of my children. Here are some needs I have seen surface again and again in my home and elsewhere:

1. To feel safe and that life is predictable
2. To give and receive love and affection
3. To be heard and understood
4. To play, learn, and experiment
5. To have free will and autonomy
6. To be capable and contribute

I have seen my own kids and other children completely and genuinely shift their behavior for the better when I or another caregiver understood how to meet their needs. People have complimented me on my children's behavior and have asked me how I am so good with children. The understanding of needs is a big part of it.

Here are ways I have met the needs my children in reference to the list above:

1. Keep the home calm and consistent. Use calm voices and respectful touching of the children. Set up and follow routines.
2. Hugs, kisses, and snuggles. Read books together. Play together. Dance together.
3. Listen attentively to my children by facing them, giving my attention, leaning forward, making eye contact, asking genuine questions and being curious about what they are saying. Validate them and their feelings.
4. Set up spaces where kids can play freely without being managed or corrected. Allow my kids to make a mess. Provide lots of outside play time and physical activity. I also teach my kids to use tools.
5. Offer choices. Ask for input or advice. Involve them in decisions about their life. When I play with my children, I often let them lead the play. I also teach my children that they are in control of their bodies by asking them if they'd like a hug…and then respecting their answer.
6. Give responsibility and ask for help taking care of the home. Have patience and encourage them when they are taking on new responsibilities and learning new skills.

Questions:

1. Can you think of any other needs and ways to meet them? Can you think of additional ways to meet the needs mentioned above?

2. Try rewording the following negative judgments into positive statements that consider genuine needs and allow for understanding.

- My child is manipulating me. He is sneaky. He is messing with me.
- He is being intentionally defiant.
- My child is lazy.
- My child makes me angry. My child made me yell at him/her.
- My child is disrespectful.
- My child should be doing X. My life should be like X. Things should be different.

Curiosity Made Me Less Reactive

Conflict happened less and less as I understood my children more. I took things less personally when I could see the world from their perspective. Not only did it make me less reactive, but this new perspective made me more skillful in helping to resolve issues. My curiosity about my children and their needs put me in a solution-finding mindset rather than a blaming and problem-finding mindset. So, put your Sherlock Holmes hat on and ask these questions often:

> "What's *really* going on here?"
> "How can I help my child?"
> "What do they really need right now?"

I understand that meeting the needs of your children might seem like a diminishment of your natural authority. I used to think that my kids should work around me, not the other way around. I can see how the alternative I'm suggesting might feel like it puts too much of a focus on children and allows them to share too much power.

I used to think: *People who cater to their children raise entitled children.* It also seemed like work, like one more thing to add to my already long list of things to do. I was busy; I didn't want more work. I know better now. In fact, I have experienced the benefits of understanding the needs of my children and can attest that it saves time and energy and also raises respectful and responsible children.

Understanding my children and what makes them tick was a huge step forward for me in being able to calm down and parent them well. Understanding them gave me a focus and something to act on. Understanding them allowed me to communicate with them, help them, and guide them. Problems got resolved quickly and with much less drama.

I became calmer and more constructive when my thinking shifted from judging and labelling them to trying to understand them. My perspective on "misbehavior" completely changed as I learned that every behavior happens for a reason and that needs are behind those reasons. Misbehavior will happen much less as you regularly meet the needs of your children. It's important to remember that children will seek needs like attention and autonomy in constructive or destructive ways. Let's help them choose well and be successful.

Help Your Children Become Emotionally Intelligent

This book focuses on the maturity and self-regulation of the parent as the most important thing, and it *is* the most important thing. However, as we gain regulation of ourselves, teaching our children the skills of emotional intelligence can contribute *even more* to a peaceful and enjoyable home. Teach your children the same things you have learned from this book. Imagine, emotionally intelligent parents and children working together!

You can start by helping your kids with their own Self awareness. Do this by normalizing talking about emotions and feelings in the body. Talk to your kids about feelings and sensations in your body and theirs. Help them tie emotions to feelings in their bodies.

Regularly engaging your children in talks about how they feel has the benefit of improving your children's emotional vocabulary and allows them to feel connected to you. If we talk about it and practice identifying emotions during neutral times, there is a higher likelihood that skill will be there for parent and child when things get more challenging. Here are some strategies that helped me teach my kids about self-awareness and EI.

- Ask them regularly about their emotions and feelings in their bodies: "How are you feeling?" "Do you feel that in your body anywhere? "How strong is it?"
- "Notice and reflect their emotions without judgment: "You seem frustrated." "You seem upset." "You seem happy."
- Take guesses about how they feel: "Are you feeling angry because…"
- Use the Wheel of Emotions to help them, or other props for young ones such as stuffed animals, emojis or cartoon depictions of faces with emotions on them
- Listen to your kids. Offer them space to speak and encourage your child to share and be expressive. On the other hand, don't tell them that they should not be feeling a certain way.

- Thank your child for sharing with you and let them know that it helps you understand them.
- Ask them about how others might be feeling. For example, you can ask about how they think siblings, friends, or characters in books are feeling.
- Talk through strong emotional experiences. Get your child's perspective regarding what happened and what they were thinking and feeling during the experience. Doing this in a calm and loving way can help them accept and normalize their emotions, make sense of the experience, and can also give them a chance to reflect on their own behavior choices.
- Support learning by encouraging reflection of how things might go differently next time: "What do you think you could do next time?"
- Encourage kids to reflect on moments where they become aware of themselves and choose to regulate themselves. "Hey, I noticed that you ended up calming down, how did you do that?"
- Notice and congratulate them when they make gains, even small gains. For example: "You got upset because you wanted X and you couldn't have it right away. I noticed that you took a break and took some breaths so you could calm down. Good for you. You did that." (I focus on the child and what the child did as opposed to what I think of it)
- Have lots of patience. EI develops over time because of both developmental maturation and accumulated experiences.

Maturely Deal with Conflict

"You don't have to join every circus that comes to town."
—Anonymous

Conflict is a Choice

Conflict can either be constructive or destructive. Conflict and disagreement can be done well and can strengthen a relationship. It can also be done poorly and lead to disconnection, anger, and resentment. The kind of conflict you engage in is a choice.

Toxic conflict happens when we get dysregulated and see the other as a threat, like the enemy. The game becomes to make the other person wrong or to hurt them somehow. No real listening happens. It's mostly about digging heels, point-proving, and in the case of children, punishing. It's a horrible game to play that leads to ruptured relationships.

However, this kind of fight or power struggle cannot be sustained by one party. It takes two to have a fight. If one person disengages and focuses on his/her calm, the fire will die down. When I look at it this way, I can see that conflict has been more of a choice than I would like to admit.

In the past, I thought that conflict had to be a win lose. I also was convinced that it also was out of my control. Oftentimes, I would catch myself shouting at my child and wonder how I ended up there. A disempowered mindset had me believing that the shouting or argument "just happened" because of circumstance.

Sometimes, I went so far as to think that it was my child who forced me into this position. "I had no choice but to behave like this. He forced me to." It sounds strange to me now that I once believed my child could have forced me to do anything. I was giving away my personal power and my responsibility. We are always the ones choosing our actions. As parents, it is important to know this and to model this.

Ultimately, I realized the harm to the home environment this was causing. So, I decided to completely op out of that toxic kind of conflict. I drew a line in the sand. I said, "No more." I bit my lip. I walked away if I had to. I practiced self-regulation and self-care. Additionally, I told everyone in the family what I was going to do and asked them to join me in opting out. It's just not worth it going down the dark road of toxic conflict.

Questions:

1. Conflict is going to happen. However, if it turns toxic, who should be the one to disengage first? Why?

2. Are you willing to opt out of toxic conflict?

3. How can you disengage from conflict in a way that still allows for respect and connection to be maintained?

Exercise: What's the Signal?

Create a game plan for the next time you notice yourself or your family slipping into a hurtful kind of conflict. Enlist your partner's, and even your children's, help. Have a conversation with them. How are you going to take a break from each other, or the conflict, and regroup so that more positive outcomes are possible? Perhaps you could use a code word or action that means disengage, breathe, and take a break.

Prevention is the Best Medicine (Before it Becomes Toxic Conflict)

The real key for me was to do the self-awareness, self-regulation, and self-care work that I've already mentioned. I'd rarely lose control of my emotions when I did those things. As a result, I was better able to deal with my kids maturely, even when emotions were heightened.

The opposite was also true. When I forgot about my emotions, and my needs and values, I'd get bothered and lose focus. Then, hurtful conflict would happen more easily. For example, when I was stretched too thin and didn't take care of myself, I noticed that I became more judgmental and reactive. From this place, it seemed as though a destructive kind of conflict was inevitable. This points to how important managing self-awareness, self-regulation and self-care is.

A similar thing would happen if my children's tanks were low. If I went too long without paying attention to them and their needs, I could tell. They would show me with their behavior that they needed something. So much of the work to mitigate conflict is pre-emptive and maintenance type work. So much conflict is avoided, or quickly resolved, when we simply restore connection and pay attention to needs, our own as well as those of our children.

Questions:

1. What is most necessary for you to get ahead of the curve and head toxic conflict off at the pass? What pre-emptive things would be good for you to do?

2. Are you willing to do these pre-emptive things? Why is it so important for you to do them?

3. If you don't opt out of toxic conflict and you continue with it, what is the short- and long-term impact on you, your family, and your children?

Constructive Conflict Between Child and Parent

Even with the best of plans and lots of preventive maintenance, conflict will still happen. How we deal with it is what matters. Conflict without upset or anger ends up looking a lot more like a reasonable discussion. It's the heightened emotions and blame that turn conflict into a fight or power struggle.

It is the upset and emotion that make conflict so hard to deal with. When people get upset, they cannot think well and communicate well. In his book, Emotional Intelligence, Daniel Goleman talks about how in really threatening or upsetting situations, the part of your brain responsible for emotions called the amygdala gets "hijacked" and activates your stress response. The amygdala disables the frontal lobes of your brain that are responsible for more rational thinking and behavior while simultaneously activating the fight-or-flight response. When this happens rational discussion and problem solving become difficult if not impossible.

As you can see, the number 1 goal if you want to do conflict more constructively would be to manage the emotion around it. First you manage your own, then you help your child manage theirs. Then, you problem solve. That's it! This is how conflict is done well.

When I notice that my child and I are in a conflict with the emotion rising I do the following:

I **Calm** Myself: I think to myself; "I am safe. I can handle this. Show your child what calm looks like."

I **Connect** with my Child: I make eye contact. I smile gently. If welcomed, I touch an arm, I give a hug. I show empathy with my face and body.

I get **Curious:** I think, "I wonder what's going on for my child. I wonder how they are feeling?"

I **Label** emotions: I say, "It seems like you are _____ (angry, sad, frustrated)."

I **Give Space for my child to speak:** After I label the emotion. I take a pause from speaking and I listen.

I **Reflect and Empathize** with what I hear: "You are mad. You wanted X and that didn't happen." That does sound upsetting/hard/frustrating/disappointing.

I **Give More Space:** I breathe and listen.

I **Validate:** I say, "I understand. That makes sense. I can see why you are upset."

I **Give More Space**: I breathe and listen. I wait for some visible signs of calming.

I **Support and/or Empower**: I say, "How can I help you? What do you think you can do now? What is the next step? What do you think a good solution for everyone is"?

I Work with my Child: Together we find a solution. I guide the process so that it is safe, healthy, and constructive. I can set a limit by giving two acceptable choices or brainstorming an alternative. I can say, "I'm sorry, you can't do that. That is not safe. You can do this or this. Which one would you like"? "I'm sorry. You can't have this, but let's think of something else."

I wanted to give a quick reference and some verbiage to the process so that you could see some of the actual words I use. However, this is not an exact script to follow. Don't feel the need to copy this. Use it as a reference. Practice it. Adapt it as you see fit. Make it your own. Take what is helpful.

Emotion Coaching is a Skill that Brings Peace

Above is the short form, a quick reference for how strong emotions can be managed well. Because of the importance of this skill, I am going to reiterate and expand a bit more below. This is a skill that can take your home from being loud, angry, and disconnected to feeling more calm, positive, and connected. It's huge.

But first I want to mention something. I do not use this for every little situation, especially now. As I have gained more connection, and the respect and trust of my children, there are fewer moments that require full blown emotion coaching. Each part of the emotion coaching is a tool that is effective on its own. For example, sometimes it's just a hug that is needed. Sometimes it's just asking, "How can I help you here?" Sometimes it's just silently being present and empathetic as my child works through something on their own.

With that said, here is a fuller explanation of what I do. As soon as I notice we are in a conflict or power struggle, I disengage from that kind of energy, but I remain present and aware of myself. I immediately take a conscious breath, knowing that reactivity is not my friend. If I recognize an uptick in my emotion or my child's emotion, I immediately use it as a cue to breathe, using deep long slow belly breaths. In this moment, staying calm is my #1 job. I don't use any strong words or make any big movements.

Using my son as an example. I let him be upset. I just allow it. It is okay for him to be upset. I know it will not last forever. In fact, if I allow for it and stay calm, it will help him calm down much faster than if I get dysregulated. I allow for verbal and physical expression of anger. I allow their bodies to move if they want. I make myself safe and allow for their expression. If I have not made it clear before, I let my child know that it's okay to be upset/angry/sad or whatever they are experiencing.

I tell myself that I am safe, I am okay, and that I am separate from him. His upset is about him, not me. I tell myself not to take his upset personally. I am the adult. I am the parent. I am here to help him.

I stay non-judgmental. Imagine how you would be present and hold space for a friend who was really upset. Could you be that present, non-judgmental, and calm for your child? Can you convey your concern and empathy with your face and energy?

I make eye contact and let my child see me breathing and being calm. In this way, I take advantage of the mirror neurons. Also, I am making it clear that *I am okay* and that their upset is not a problem for me. I am a source of safety. I think a lot of conflict escalates when a child reacts to the parent reacting to the child's original upset. Ha! Does that make sense?

I ask my child to breathe with me if they will. If not, I don't push it. I just model it.

I offer a hug, "Can I give you a hug?" (I respect a no if it's a no.)

I get curious and try to understand what he is going through and how I can help. What is he trying to communicate? Is there a need to be met? I get ready to listen.

After some time, when the child has calmed down a bit, I help him identify how he is feeling. I do not do that until the child has visibly calmed down a bit. Asking a child to engage in conversation about the emotional state while they are still emotionally heightened has backfired for many parents. Saying "Use your words" to an upset child can be kind of condescending, if not ineffective.

I help identify the emotion. "It seems like you are frustrated." "Are you feeling angry?" The first option I mention is an observation. The second option is a genuine guess. I have used either one at different times depending on the child and the situation. Children who might not be able to answer the question directly could benefit from the support of a parent making a genuine guess.

Sometimes I ask my kids where they feel the emotion in their body and what kind of sensation is present in that place, and how strong it is. I do this because emotions are often linked to body sensations. It helps with self-awareness.

Once the child himself expresses how he feels, I reflect the feeling and paraphrase what I understand to be the reason. For example, "You are mad. You want to ride in the car, but not in your car seat." If I have gotten it right, the child might agree and might also add some more context. If I haven't gotten it exactly right, the child will likely correct me and might add some more context. I just listen.

Then I validate his feelings. "I understand. You don't like the straps and the way they feel. (I nod) I get it. I understand what you are saying." At some point, you might notice a relaxing of the child's body. To be fully empathized with and validated is a powerful thing. To not be judged, but fully accepted feels supportive and connecting. (I might offer another hug here).

When I get to this point, it feels like we are on the same team. I have helped him calm down and established some connection. I have listened instead of immediately correcting or blaming.

This is when I start facilitating the solution-finding process, not before. High emotion and problem-solving don't go well together. I ask some questions in a positive tone like "How can I help you here?" "What would you like?" "What do you think we could do?" These questions allow you to have a conversation, and to further understand what is going on for your child. These genuine questions continue to build trust and connection. I believe that a child experiences this as very safe and reassuring when a parent genuinely tries to understand and solve the problem WITH them.

I don't try to stop them from thinking a certain way. I don't dismiss or negate potential ideas. You don't need to make them wrong for wanting what they want. However, you don't need to agree either. Even if my child initially says, "I want to ride in the car with no car seat," I stay calm and nod. I might say, "Okay, that's an idea." I help them consider the pros and cons of it. This considering and discussing the child's ideas further validates them and brings them into the fold of the solution-finding process. It also results in cooperation. Yes, this might take longer at first, but it results in solutions that are longer lasting.

I don't make the problem into a power battle. I don't make the problem about my child's behavior either. I put the problem in front of us rather than between us and calmly facilitate a solution together. I can do this because I'm the adult! Obviously, I'm not going to let my child ride in the car without a car seat. Helping him calm down, understand how he is feeling, understanding the bigger picture, and learning how to collaborate are the real lessons at play here.

As the parent, you facilitate the conversation so there is never a need to feel out of control. You'd be surprised how many children rise to the challenge of collaborating or solving the problem in a completely reasonable and positive way. This kind of solution-finding is very effective in satisfying the needs of being heard and being autonomous. It is ultimately empowering to the child, and it helps them develop their own problem-solving skills. Not every conversation ends in agreement. A parent may have to establish a limit. This might be hard for your child to take. That's okay. Limits are upsetting sometimes. However, now you know how to deal with upset. Go back to step 1 if you need to and repeat the process.

Dealing with Conflict Between Siblings

Not all conflict happens between parent and child. Some parents have a harder time dealing with the conflict between children. Because of their discomfort with conflict and the difficult feelings that arise inside of themselves, parents can rush to quickly solve or shut down the conflict between the children, acting as a referee. This is a short-term solution that doesn't allow for connection, learning, or empowerment.

I want to teach and empower my children so that, as the years go by, I am needed less and less to resolve a situation, and the kids become more and more capable of doing this for themselves. This is mentorship and leadership in action.

Below is a process that I use that describes the example of a brother hitting a sister to get her attention. I adapted this from the work of Dr. Becky Bailey and Dr. Laura Markham. Their respective work is amazing and is changing homes and school environments for the better. I have added some of my own understanding or verbiage to their processes

1. Make yourself Safe and be a Model for Calm

The first order of business is to check in with your own emotions and recognize what you are feeling. Many parents get upset when one of their children gets upset. Emotions can be contagious. Parents can have a knee-jerk reaction to conflict because of this "emotional contagion." Parents can heighten an already frantic situation by allowing themselves to be emotionally influenced by their children's upset. Be wary of taking on the distress of your children. It tends to put you in a mental, emotional, and physiological state that is not helpful. It is much harder to parent maturely from an emotionally heightened place.

- Remind yourself that you are safe, you are okay, and that you are separate from your children. Say it to yourself. (I am safe, I am okay, I am separate from them.)
- Take deep belly breaths to reinforce this mindset and to anchor this safety into your body.
- Remind yourself that modelling calm and patience is the most important thing you can do. Say it to yourself. (The most important thing I can do is to be calm and patient.)

2. Go to the "Injured Party" First

Do not punish or otherwise scold or glare at the aggressor. Do what is necessary to help everyone be safe. But do so in a calm way, and do not rush to lay blame or attempt to fix the situation.

"Be with" and empathize with the Injured party:

- Sit with the child in their hurt. Look at the child with love. Breathe. Tell the child with your eyes that you understand how he/she feels. Get close. Place a hand on the child if it's welcomed.

- Refrain from talking a lot, if at all. Many parents talk a lot during the initial moments of conflict...whether they are lecturing the aggressor or asking the injured party if they are okay. These are rarely helpful and can add to the overwhelm and distress.
- Let your child see your empathetic face and let them see your breathing and your calm. They will eventually follow suit.
- You can ask if they would like a hug.

Empower the Injured party:

- "You seem sad and angry." (Pause and let your child speak if she wants)
- "You didn't like it when your brother hit you." (Pause and let your child speak if she wants)
- "Look at your brother and tell him that you didn't like it. You can say, "I didn't like it when you hit me. Say it now". After she says it... Let this hang in the air a bit. The aim here is to give a voice to the injured party and to help the aggressor understand his impact.
- "I think your brother wanted your attention. Next time he wants your attention, what can he do instead of hitting you. Tell him what he can do instead".
- "Okay, you want him to tap you on your shoulder and say your name. Great. Tell him that next time he wants your attention to tap you on your shoulder and say your name." "Say it now."

3. Teach the Aggressor Empathy and Communication Skills

- "You seem upset too. Can I give you a hug?"
- "Did you want your sister to pay attention to you?" "Did you want to tell her something?"

- "You didn't know what else to do so you hit her. Is that right?"
- "Did your sister like it when you hit her? How do you think she felt? Look at her face, what is her face saying?" (Ask these questions with a neutral, non-shaming tone)
- Let this land a bit. Give it some time to hang in the air. This is where empathy gets internalized. This is where a child can understand the impact of his actions. In a non-judgmental and non-punitive environment, a child is free to access empathy. With blaming and yelling, empathy does not occur, only shaming.
- Is there anything you want to say or do for her?
- "Next time you want your sister to pay attention, what can you do instead? What did she say?" "Yes, okay. You can tap her on the shoulder, say her name and say excuse me."
- "Let's practice it now." (Have a do-over)
- "Great. You both did it." "Did that feel better?"

Two "Injured Parties"

This approach works even if both parties feel like the injured party. There doesn't have to be a clear "aggressor" and "victim". If both children feel hurt, then do the process twice, taking turns with each child occupying each role. This approach can also be used if the parent feels like the injured party. You can simply state in a positive and assertive voice for example, "I don't like it when you hit me. If you want my attention, please tap me on my leg like this and say excuse me Mom/Dad."

Side note: Don't be surprised if after you teach this approach, and use it, your children use it when they feel hurt or they feel like you are being an aggressor. Don't be surprised if you hear from your child at some point, "Mom/Dad I don't like it when you yell at me. If you want my attention, could you please talk to me kindly?"

Questions

1. How would you react if your child was assertive with you and told you what they liked and didn't like and asked you to change the way you approached them?

2. Do you think this kind of assertiveness could serve your children well in their lives? If so, how?

The Purpose Behind This Approach

The main reason I like this approach is because it is aimed at helping children find their voice and resolve their own conflict. There is a greater likelihood that children who are mentored and taught skills like this will be able to help themselves, now, and throughout their lives. The aim is to encourage empathy, as opposed to punishment, as a means of managing behavior. Developing an internal compass is a far greater motivator for prosocial behavior than punishing.

I understand that parents might think that it's necessary to punish the aggressor right away. This was often my first reaction. However, this does not teach the child to tap into his/her own empathy. It also does not teach the skill needed to handle conflict the next time it occurs. The child is left feeling bad and ashamed but doesn't acquire any skills to do better next time. This can create a vicious cycle of an unskilled child getting more and more frustrated due to his inability to communicate, while also dealing with increasing feelings of shame and disconnection.

Without the teaching of skills, the injured party is also left without an idea of how to help themself next time. They learn to rely on the intervention of the parent. Years of this kind of approach can lead to disempowerment of the child.

In the above examples, I used potential safety concerns as the points of conflict: getting into a car seat and hitting a sibling. I did this on purpose. Both situations could justify a certain reactive response from a parent since "safety is on the line". I used to use safety concerns as a trump card for me to get angry. The safety factor allowed me to give myself permission to be reactive. Or at least, this is what I told myself. Some situations are in fact dangerous enough that a swift and loud response is necessary. However, those situations are rare, and these two examples do not qualify.

I know that the above processes might seem long and tedious, even laughable to some. I get it. There would have been a time that I would have laughed at them. But that would have been the part of me that was impatient, ego-driven, and ill-informed.

Understanding what I do now, about children and parenting, I know that a big part of our job is to holistically prepare our kids well for life. We cannot do this by power-tripping, scolding, or even by fixing all their problems for them. We must stay calm and patient enough so that we can include the child in the solution-finding process. They cannot learn if we do not involve them.

Cruise Control Kind of Parenting

Yelling, being reactive, punishing, or quickly resolving a situation by playing the part of the referee or bully are all short-term fixes. And they guarantee that you will be kept busy for the rest of your days as a parent. Maybe I am lazy, but I do not want to spend the rest of my parenting days running around putting out fires and yelling. I like to be relaxed at home. I don't really like hearing my voice repeatedly, either.

The way of parenting I propose is similar to delayed gratification. It requires that you delay your immediate "desire" of how you are conditioned to react. It requires that you control yourself and any knee-jerk reactions to stop and/or resolve the conflict. It also means that you model calm, solution-finding behavior. If you are mindful now and choose smarter, more self-disciplined parenting actions that teach and build skills, it will pay great dividends later, and you will reap the rewards.

Initially, this process will take longer. However, the good news is that eventually your kids won't need to rely on you to solve everything for them. They will know how to stay calm and will have the tools to find resolution themselves. A calm home is the reward.

Being calm, modeling calm, empathizing, and then solution finding is the holy grail of parenting. When I demonstrated this consistently enough, I saw that my children started to follow suit. It is worth it to adopt a long view of parenting and use a conflict resolution process like this. It is worth it not only for the peace that it brings to your home, but also for the real-life skill development of your children.

Questions

1. How do you think it could benefit your child to learn calm and mature ways of dealing with conflict in his/her life?

2. How do you think it would benefit the home environment to learn and use a mature conflict resolution process?

Practice Self-Compassion and Forgiveness

"If we are facing in the right direction, all
we have to do is keep on walking."
—Buddhist expression

Stick with It

I made a gamble at the beginning of this journey by focusing on my own actions and learning to regulate myself in the hopes that it would have a positive effect on my family. It was a good bet to make. It has completely paid off, and I believe it has altered my family's trajectory in the best of ways. It wasn't an easy gamble to take, though.

My habits and background told me that I should be doing the opposite, that I should be focusing on and fixing my children's behaviors. There was social pressure, too. Some friends and family questioned me and my thinking. They were concerned that I'd raise entitled or spoiled children if I didn't give my kids tough love. I totally understand this concern.

There was a big part of me that felt the same way. However, since then, I've learned that harshness isn't necessary. In fact, it's counterproductive. I've learned that staying calm allows *more* lessons to be learned. Calm/conscious/positive parenting doesn't mean that there can't be rules, responsibilities, or limits. I had to stick with it long enough to see the results from this more encouraging way of parenting.

There were many times I wanted to give up and go back to how I used to parent. There were times that I did give up and gave into my anger. Again and again, I had to come back to a commitment I made to be a better dad, a commitment that involved being 100 percent responsible and accountable for my actions.

Full Ownership

Yes, owning my behavior was challenging and humbling. However, it has also led to so much positive transformation that it has been unquestionably worth it. Additionally, it has modeled personal responsibility for my kids. For example, when my children apologize for hurting each other, it is from a place of awareness and empathy, not from obligation.

The way I live shows them that I am responsible for myself and my actions. I am in control of my behavior. I am in control of my life. If I make a mistake or hurt someone, it is my responsibility to step up and repair the relationship.

These are the messages that full ownership sends. These are the lessons that children learn when we act like this. It feels vulnerable, yet brave, at the same time. Deep down, I think we all want to take full ownership of our lives. Living and parenting from this place has made me finally feel like a mature human and parent.

Self-Compassion

There's a necessary counterbalance to the commitment to full ownership. It's a commitment to self-compassion. You see, people who are hard on their kids are often hard on themselves. They do not easily accept or forgive themselves, or at least I didn't. I didn't easily move on from mistakes. I was my own worst critic.

Acknowledging and addressing a mistake is important but defining ourselves by our mistakes is neither helpful nor true. We are not bad people because of our mistakes. We all make mistakes from time to time, but deep down most of us are honestly trying to lead a good life.

Self-compassion and forgiveness allow us to recognize our inner goodness and recognize that we are indeed trying. I found that full ownership without forgiveness was too harsh and demotivating. I had to allow myself to be human.

What I know to be true now, is that the acceptance I have for myself closely reflects the acceptance I have for my kids. When I softened and became more compassionate with myself, I did the same with my kids.

Self-compassion allowed me to keep the momentum going in the right direction. I knew that I needed every bit of motivation to overcome my autopilot parenting.

As a result, I use all the resources I have to create a better environment for my kids. I've stopped spending my energy blaming and judging myself. It was a tough balance to strike: to be better than I was yesterday, and to forgive myself when I came up short.

I still make mistakes. The only difference now is that I don't let negative energy from these mistakes consume me. I do the opposite. I use the energy to be better.

Instead of fixating on a misstep, I do what I can to fix it and then use the opportunity to recommit myself to my vision and to meaningful action that will move me in that direction. It's almost as if I use my mistakes as reminders, as cues to push me toward my goals. I set it up so everything moves me in the direction I want to go. Creating a home of compassion and forgiveness is so much more enjoyable than one of judgement and negativity.

Exercise: Self-Compassion

1. What are some judgments you have of yourself and the way that you parent? Reword each of those judgments into statements that are more understanding, compassionate, accurate, and take into consideration where you have come from.

2. Think about a time when a friend was having a hard time and you were there to support. How did you respond to your friend in this situation? How were you present for him or her? What did you say? What was your tone?

3. Would you be willing to treat yourself like a close friend? How would it sound to do that in response to a mistake you made in parenting? Write a letter to yourself and show yourself that you understand the struggles you are going through.

Here is an example of me rewording a judgment.

The judgement: You are a bad parent. You are aggressive, you always yell, and you are not getting any better. You should be better.

The compassionate truth: You are trying to be a better parent. You are learning how to be more encouraging and patient. You care a lot about your children, and you are making improvements.

Here is a letter I wrote where I was empathetic, validating, and compassionate...to me. You can use this example to help you write your own letter.

> Drew, it sounds like you are having a hard time with your kids. You are reacting in ways that you wish you hadn't. I'm sorry. That sounds frustrating. You seem upset. You want to do better. You want so badly to be in control of yourself and be a good example for your children. You're super frustrated. You are sad too, and tired. I get it. That makes sense. I understand why you'd feel like that.
> (Take a Deep Breath with me)
>
> You really want to do better. You are trying hard and still making mistakes. This is challenging for you. Parenting feels hard. You just want to be done with all the struggles and for you to have full control of yourself...and to have a peaceful home. Did I get it? Did I get how you were feeling? Is there anything else?
>
> (Can I give you a hug?) - I might even hug myself here.
>
> Can I offer you a different perspective? Are you up for that? Can I tell you what I see?
>
> Okay. I see a guy who is trying hard, who cares a lot about his children and how he is affecting them. I see a guy who has made

improvements. You have come a long way, really. Look at where you started. Look where you are now. You are doing it. It makes sense to me that you are having a hard time. You never studied or practiced how to parent. This is all new, and it's challenging. There is a lot to learn about children, childhood development, and emotional management. This is a complex skill set. To do this job well requires a lot of poise, composure, and practice.

I want to let you know that I see you. I know this is hard for you. And I also want you to know that you are on your way. That's what I see. I see your effort. This is a journey. You are on the path. Yes, you are going to make mistakes from time to time. You are human. We all make mistakes. Would you be willing to accept yourself as human and acceptable even when you make mistakes? You would? Cool. Ha. Welcome to your humanity. I believe in you. I've got your back.

I love you

Drew

Forgiveness

Throughout my life, I have tried to find motivation for doing things by being hard on myself. In this case, however, I noticed that blaming and judging myself didn't help me with my parenting, nor did it help me move in the direction I wanted to go. In fact, it made things worse. Being too hard on myself would send me into a shame spiral. Motivating myself to become a better parent through self-criticism did not actually work. And I don't think it works that well in other situations either.

This helped me see the logic behind why blaming and shaming didn't help my kids either. With my increased awareness, I'd catch myself and think, *I wouldn't like to be spoken to like this, so why am I talking to my children like this?* Seeing myself as human allowed me to see my kids as human, and vice versa. Now, the message in our home is that we all make mistakes, yet we are all loveable and forgivable.

Now when I mess up, I genuinely apologize and move on. I don't dwell on it. My family has followed suit and the environment is so much better as a result. A loving and forgiving home is so much better than a judgmental and critical home. If you have also noticed that constant correcting, blaming, and shaming hasn't been a great motivator to do the right thing, then I would suggest letting it go and practicing loving yourself (and your family) instead.

I use mistakes now as opportunities to be curious about myself and how I can grow. Just like I do with my kids, when my behavior gets reactive, I ask myself, "What was really going on there for you Drew? What led you to act like that? What do you need? How can I help"? I try to treat that scared or angry part of myself like a good parent would treat a child in distress.

So, let's all love and accept ourselves as human. When we know that we are good, yet fallible, forgiveness comes much easier. Judgment can't exist when forgiveness is present. The forgiveness I have been able to find for myself has strengthened my ability to offer it to my children.

Exercise: Do-Over

1. Think of a parenting situation that challenged you. Discuss how you behaved in response to it. How could

you have responded in a more emotionally intelligent way? If you had been able to regulate yourself better, what would the outcome have been? Why is this important?

2. Role play a new version of this situation with your spouse or friend. Have fun and play with it. Get into it, especially the person who is playing the child. Parents, focus on the self-management skills you have learned. The goal is to stay calm and in control of yourself. What was the result? Was it difficult? What were the thoughts you were thinking?

3. Think of a mistake you made with your child. Go back to your child and tell them you made a mistake. Apologize and ask if you can have a do-over to do what you think would have been better. Complete the do-over. Pay attention to giving a genuine apology that has no strings attached. Own your actions without shifting responsibility for your actions onto your child. Do not give a backhanded apology. For example, don't do this: "I am sorry that I hurt you, but you were being so rude and loud that I had to grab you hard and stop you…" In fact, rewording an apology that was phrased that way can be its own kind of do-over.

Recognize Your Efforts

There will be times when you make mistakes. In these moments, you have a choice to make. You can give yourself compassion or judgment. I'm hoping that you choose compassion for you and your children. You have the same opportunity when someone else makes a mistake: will your response be compassionate or punitive?

My other piece of advice is to celebrate wins. If there are times when you notice you're breaking a cycle or choosing a better path, then celebrate. Celebrate with yourself, your spouse, or friends. Talk to someone. Be proud of yourself and the fact that your efforts are paying off.

The fact that you are trying to improve is worthy of mention. Not everyone puts in an effort like this. Self-examination and improvement are hard. The fact that you made it this far says something about you. Recognizing effort and progress is often hard for people who are hard on themselves. But this is part of self-acceptance, too.

If we are big enough to own our shortcomings, then we must be big enough to own our effort and progress. You are trying. That is enough, and you are enough. You are in a different spot than you used to be! You are charting a new course and the entire trajectory of your life, and your family will be better off as a result. This is big news. *Things are changing for the better because of you!*

Exercise: Create a Success Journal:

Journal your wins. Whenever you catch yourself acting in a more mature way, document it, even the smallest of things. This can be a powerful exercise. Parents who are hard on their kids are often hard on themselves. Instead of constantly moving the finish line forward and not feeling good enough, this exercise allows you to document progress. It allows you to have a reference point for your improvement. It allows you to see where you have come from. It also allows you to pick up your journal from time to time and just feel good about the progress you've made.

GOODBYE AND GOOD LUCK

You can do this. You can create a calm and loving home. I believe in you. If I can do it, so can you. It is worth it, please believe me. Even though this journey was hard for me, and still can be, I would not trade it for the world. It is rewarding to know that I am doing the best that I can so that my kids can have the best chance to grow up happy and healthy.

I hope this book has been helpful. If it has, let me know. Email me, message me, tell me your story. I would love to hear from you.

If you are still struggling after reading this book, I can recommend a few things. Read the book again, slow down, and do the exercises more completely. Take your time to do each activity and to journal and write everything down. If you worked your way through this book alone, do it again with someone else (or a group) and share your answers and reflections with each other. The next thing I can recommend would be to get some support. Perhaps you would benefit from some professional support in your life.

There are nuances to all of this and there are also things that I've likely forgotten to include in the book, or perspectives I simply don't have. If it seems like there could be more tools and strategies to learn, that's because there are. This book does not cover all of parenting. I've given you what I know are the most powerful perspectives and tools so that you can overcome anger to create a calmer and more loving home. This is what I shared because it was my journey and because I believe it is the foundation and gateway to many other good things in parenting.

Each parent and each family are unique, and each situation is unique. I had to puzzle through what worked for me and what didn't. I had to learn about myself and really feel into what worked for me. I had to experiment, observe, and adjust. I encourage you to do the same.

This journey is not a straight line. This work is not like a pill you can swallow. It takes time and patience, for you and your children. Parenting is a long game, and it requires that you stay focused on your intentions, and willing to recommit when you fall off track.

If you would like further support, I have a one-on-one private coaching practice. I also provide a parenting course. You can contact me at drewtupper.com. Reading books is great. It can get you started. But, in my experience, support is needed.

I feel grateful to have helped so many parents overcome anger, reactivity, and inconsistency to become more patient, loving, and consistent with their children. The results have been wonderful. I feel really honored to do the work that I do.

It is so rewarding to see parents become the type of parents they want to be, to see relationships restored, and to see more healthy and empowered children in the world. It's exciting to me to think about the ripple effect of it all. I imagine those children eventually having children, and so on, and what a positive environment we can create for generations to come.

Because the journey never ends, and because learning never ends, I will leave you with a few books by teachers and researchers that I respect. I have learned a great deal from these authors and parents. I recommend any video, book, or course you can find from these great teachers.

Parenting for a Peaceful World (Dr. Robin Grille)
Dare to Lead (Dr. Brené Brown)
The Conscious Parent (Dr. Shefali)
Parenting from the Inside out (Dr. Dan Seigel)
Emotional Intelligence (Dr. Daniel Goleman)
The Body Keeps Score (Dr. Bessel van der Kolk)
Healing Trauma (Dr. Peter Levine)
Conscious Discipline (Dr. Becky Bailey)
Playful Parenting (Dr. Lawrence J. Cohen)

Goodbye and Good luck!

With love and respect,

Drew

ABOUT THE AUTHOR

 Drew is here on this Earth to experience life, to love and to learn. He is passionate about parenting and conscious relating.

Home is on beautiful Vancouver Island where the family enjoys playing, laughing and adventuring together.

Drew is a certified teacher, a parenting coach and student to his greatest teachers, his children. They have taught him the most important lessons of all. He knows that parenting is the most important job in the world and that how we parent paves the way for our collective future.

Follow Drew on Facebook or Instagram @drewtupper

Printed in Great Britain
by Amazon

87247477R00070